KB160165

Big Fat Cat

AND THE

FORTUNE COOKIE

Takahiko Mukoyama

Tetsuo Takashima

with studio ET CETERA

월북

• 영어를 이해하는 데 굳이 번역문은 필요하지 않다는 저자의 뜻에 따라 우리말 해석을 싣지 않았습니다. 하지만 이 책을 다 본 후에 정확한 번역을 확인하고 싶다면 윌북 영어 카페에 들러주세요. 언제든 환영합니다.
cafe.naver.com/everville

ビッグ・ファット・キャットとフォーチュン・クッキー
BIG FAT CAT AND THE FORTUNE COOKIE

Copyright © 2004 by Takahiko Mukoyama and Tetsuo Takashima

Korean translation copyright © 2014 by Will Books Publishing Co.
Korean translation rights arranged with GENTOSHA Inc.
through Japan UNI Agency, Inc., Tokyo and Korea Copyright Center, Inc., Seoul

이 책의 한국어판 저작권은 (주)한국저작권센터(KCC)를 통한
저작권자와의 독점계약으로 도서출판 윌북에 있습니다.
저작권법에 의해 한국 내에서 보호를 받는 저작물이므로 무단전재와 무단복제를 금합니다.

PREVIOUSLY IN THE BIG FAT CAT SERIES

충실하지 않은
Ed Wishbone and his unfaithful pet cat
(find) 할 수 있다
have finally managed to find
a new home and a new pie shop
— thanks to Professor Willy
and his homeless friends.

Now, Ed must help them back
by winning the prize money
of the State Pie Contest and
getting Professor Willy in a hospital.
But Willy is very sick and
there isn't much time...

"Yes."

"The contracts are signed. I want that street torn down by the end of next month. Yes, the one they call 'Ghost Avenue.'"

계약서

허물다

"You did well with that shopping mall in Old Everville... Yes, that Out-something Mall. Wait."

Jeremy Lightfoot Senior pressed a button on the phone and switched lines.

"Yes? I see... All right. Good. Oh, and one more thing. If my son happens to win the contest, tell the judges he was 심사위원 responsible for Wishbone's problems." 책임이 있는

실격시키다
"Yes. Disqualify him."

"Okay. How many pies now?"

The host stuck his head behind the curtain of the judges'
booth and asked a staff member. The staff member was busy
running around with pies in his hands. He shouted to the host.

"Sixteen. Almost done!"

"Okay. Time?"

"Thirty seconds and counting."

"Got it," the host said as he stepped back onto the stage.

"LADIES AND GENTLEMEN! Thirty more
seconds! Most of the pies are finished, and the battle
is coming to an end! This is Robert R. Silverman.
Welcome back to the PIEGAMES!"

"Thirty seconds!?" George looked back at Ed. "Did he say thirty seconds?!"

"Don't stop! Keep going!" Ed shouted back to George, as he shook a saucepan full of blueberries. They were the only ones still baking. Most of the other contestants were cleaning up their booths. A lot of people in the audience were laughing and pointing at them.

"Twenty seconds!" the host announced.

Ed was covered with food — whipped cream on his head, flour spread over his shirt, and blueberry stains on his sleeves.

"Ten!"

The host cried, and the audience joined in.

"Nine!" they called out together.

8

Ed's hands were shaking badly. He tried to calm down but couldn't. The whole world seemed to spin around him.

"Ed! There's no time!" George cried out in panic.

Ed dashed to the table with his saucepan. But he moved too fast. He slipped and the saucepan flew through the air.

"Five!" the crowd counted.

Ed and George both tried to catch the saucepan. They both failed. The blueberries in the saucepan scattered all over the floor. Some of them splashed on Ed.

"Three!"

Ed and George stared at each other.

"Two!"

Ed closed his eyes.

"One!"

"BeeJees?"

Frank peeked at BeeJees to check if he was asleep. He was.
Frank shrugged, and drove his wagon past BeeJees, whistling a
tune from a cartoon show.

"Yaba daba daba... Yaba daba dooo..."

Willy had finally stopped shaking a while ago, and BeeJees
had fallen asleep from exhaustion. Frank had come over to see if
he was all right.

Something cracked beneath Frank's wagon. Frank bent down and found one of Willy's fortune cookies stuck under the front wheel. He reached down and picked it up.

The fortune paper was sticking out. He pulled it out and took a look.

"Mi... Mira..."

Frank tried to read it, but gave up. He laid the paper down gently beside Willy, and went back to the fire. Some friends of Willy's had gathered a pile of wood for them. Frank started adding wood to the fire.

Unnoticed by anyone, Willy's hand moved slightly. It touched the fortune paper Frank had set beside him.

The paper reflected the flickering red light of the campfire. Once, twice, it glowed. Then a gust of wind blew it into the fire, and it disappeared forever.

"Aaaand it's over!!"

The host raised his hand and announced aloud. Most of
the contestants threw their hats and aprons up into the air and
hugged each other. The audience applauded hard and the pie
contest came to an end.

Ed was still holding the eggbeater in his hand. He had
squeezed his eyes shut and was frozen in that position. George
wanted to say something to Ed, but couldn't. All he could do was
stare at the clock tower.

Two half-finished pies lay on the table. Ed and George sat
silently on the floor as everyone else ran around them.

"Shucks," George licked the blueberry on his finger and
mumbled to himself. "And it tastes so good too."

"Wishbone."

Ed looked up. It was Jeremy Lightfoot Jr. He had taken off
his costume. He stood there staring at the unfinished pies. All
around them, the contest staff was busy getting ready for the
presentation of the pies.

Jeremy broke off a piece of Ed's unfinished pie, tasted it, and stared vacantly at the rest of the pie.

"Wishbone... About that *trouble* you had..."

Ed shook his head and got up. Purple syrup dripped from his shirt.

"It doesn't matter anymore," Ed said. "The contest's over."

He wiped blueberries off his forehead and started to walk past Jeremy. But Jeremy caught him by the arm.

"Listen, Wishbone. I need to tell you something."

Jeremy jerked Ed back. But before he could start talking, Jeremy saw the despair in Ed's eyes and closed his mouth.

"Ladies and gentlemen..." A voice from the speakers echoed above Ed's head. It was the owner of the New Mall. *"I think it's time to decide our winner."*

Ed silently took Jeremy's hand from his arm. He forced himself to smile.

"It's too late. This was the one time I couldn't fail... no matter what — but I did." Ed couldn't keep smiling any more, so he closed his eyes.

"It's over. Nothing can save us now."

Wrong.

"Holy Jesus Christ in heaven!!"

The owner almost had a heart attack as he took a look

backstage. He staggered and almost fell, but somehow kept

standing. He continued to stare at the incredible mess behind the

curtains. It looked like a miniature hurricane had run through

the pies.

After recovering from the first wave of shock, the owner

realized he was still holding the microphone in his hand. He

gulped, then spoke into it slowly.

"Um... Ladies and gentlemen, I'm... I'm really sorry. I think

there's been... *an accident backstage.*"

The owner could hear the audience stir as he said these words.

He looked around the booth again. Almost all of the pies had

been completely destroyed. He had no choice but to continue.

"Um... I'm sorry. We may have to cancel the contest."

16

The main tent had become a confused riot.

The owner and a few other staff members were trying to explain to the angry audience what had happened, but they were not succeeding. This was no surprise, because they had no idea themselves what had happened.

One staff member claimed he had seen "something like an incredibly fast bowling ball run out of the booth," but that was all they knew. The owner and the staff offered a rematch sometime next year, but that just made everyone angrier.

Ed, George, and Jeremy stood watching in silence as everyone fussed and shouted about the sudden developments. Ed took off his bandanna and stuck it in his pocket. He started to walk away.

"Where are you going, Wishbone?" Jeremy asked.

Ed didn't respond. He just walked out the back door. George and Jeremy stared at each other after the door closed.

In a corner near the judges' booth, the owner stood surrounded by angry contestants demanding a better answer. Everything was in chaos.

The contest is falling apart, Jeremy thought. *Just as Father would have wanted.*

In his mind, he heard his father laughing. Everything always seemed to end as his father had planned. He was sick and tired of it.

Jeremy walked over to the judges' booth, picked up a microphone, and switched it on.

"So why don't we do it now?"

Jeremy's voice boomed out of the speakers. Almost everyone stopped moving and talking. They all looked at Jeremy. Jeremy spoke through the microphone again.

"The rematch. Why don't we do it now?"

A long pause followed, and then one of the contestants shouted.

"Yeah, why not now?"

That was the cue. Everyone started agreeing all at once. The contestants began shouting for a rematch and the cries from the stands became even more fierce. George looked across the arena at Jeremy. Jeremy shrugged and laid down the microphone.

The owner was overwhelmed by the reaction of the crowd. He exchanged glances with the judges.

"Uh... Let us consider this for a moment, please."

The audience kept chanting "Rematch! Rematch!" over and over, louder and louder, until there was no other sound in the stadium.

"A rematch?"

Ed said to George with a bewildered look. He had been standing alone outside the main tent. George had come running over to him with the news. Ed asked again, "A rematch? Why?"

"The pies were all destroyed. They don't know why," George explained. "But everyone agreed on a second round. We're back in business, Ed!"

Ed had a look of pure surprise for a moment, but then he gradually lowered his eyes and nodded. George was almost dancing around, but he stopped when he noticed that Ed wasn't happy.

"What's the matter? We just got another chance, didn't we?"

"Yup," Ed said in a tired voice. "I know."

But he said nothing more. George looked worried.

"Are you okay? Want me to get you a cup of coffee or something?"

"Thanks. But no thanks," Ed said.

"What's wrong, man? Isn't this great news?"

Ed sighed and looked at George with a sad smile.

"George. You saw that pie we made. I was stupid to think we really had a chance to win."

George's usually happy face clouded over. Ed saw this and felt a tinge of guilt. He looked away.

"Even if I'd made the pie right, it was just a regular fruit pie. Nothing special. I'm sorry, George. You saw all those other pies. You know we don't have any chance of winning."

"But you *will* win," George said abruptly. "I know you'll win."

"George..." Ed said, hearing the sincerity in George's voice. George's trust in him was so genuine it scared him. "Thanks, but sorry. I... I'm really sorry."

Overhead, an announcement echoed from the speakers.

"...the PIEGAMES will restart at three o'clock, after a one hour break. During the break, contestants will be allowed to get extra supplies. We are very sorry for the inconvenience. If you choose not to watch the rematch, full refunds for your tickets will be..."

Ed looked away towards the Ferris wheel. George realized he was about to walk away, and tried desperately to say something to stop him — anything that would cheer him up, anything that would tell him how much George appreciated him. But this was too difficult for George. The truth was, he really believed that Ed would win. He just didn't know why.

"Ed!" George cried out helplessly.

"Your pies are the best!" he said. "The best in the world! *I know it!*" George kept shouting even after Ed had disappeared into the crowd. "Your pies are the best! I know it! I know it!"

The Ferris wheel was slowly rotating through the winter sky as Ed walked beneath it. He came to the far end of the carnival grounds and leaned on the outer fence. Hands in his pockets, he watched the Ferris wheel go around. His thoughts went around with it, around and around, almost as if he were hypnotized.

There are chances, and there are consequences.

The fortune cookie had said. He wondered whether the rematch was the chance or the consequence. He wondered if it even mattered.

You have no idea what a pie is made of.

Willy had said, but now he heard it in his own voice.

An endless stream of people walked past him. Some were families, some were couples, and some were alone. It was fascinating just to imagine all of the different lives, different problems, different feelings, and different tastes these people had.

It seemed crazy to make a pie that everyone would like. It was like finding a puzzle piece that fit every spot in the puzzle. It seemed impossible.

Ed spotted a balloon floating above the Ferris wheel. His mind wandered away with it.

Bake your pie.

Willy had said. He thought he was doing that, but now he wasn't so sure.

But I have responsibilities. I have to win.

But was that really true? Or was it just an excuse?

Your pies are the best.

George had said. And Ed had been ashamed. Because the pies he baked were really not his pies at all. He knew his pie was not as sour or sweet as a blueberry pie. It was different. It was different from anything else, and that was what frightened him — had frightened him, perhaps, for his entire life.

But he had found out that he was not the only one different.
Willy was different. Frank was different. Everyone who lived on
Ghost Avenue was different.

Ed closed his eyes. He thought about Jeremy and what he
had said. He thought about George. And mostly, he thought
about Willy.

Go, son. Bake your pie.

When he opened his eyes again, Ed was still looking up at the
balloon in the sky. It was now high up in the clouds. The Ferris
wheel continued its silent, slow movement.

You're going to be late again. You're going to fail.

The voice inside of him spoke again, but for the first time in
his life, Ed ignored it.

The balloon had disappeared far off in the clouds.

It was time to bake his pie.

George was really getting worried when the clock read 2:55 and Ed still hadn't returned to the booth. All the contestants were already in place, ready to begin. George was about to go look for Ed when Ed burst through the back door and came running up to him.

"Sorry. I lost track of time. How's the oven?"

"Red-hot and ready to go," George said with a smile.

"Okay. Get everything out of that shopping bag," Ed said, pointing to a bag on the floor. "I'll get myself ready."

While Ed grabbed an apron and wrapped a bandanna around his head, George dug into the shopping bag. He stopped when he took out a yellow bottle.

"Uh... Ed!" George yelled in astonishment. "This isn't blueberry."

George showed Ed the bottle of mustard he held in his hand.

"I know," Ed replied in a confident voice.

"Oh..." George mumbled in a dumbfounded way and started placing the bottle on the table. But he turned around a second time. "No! Ed! You don't understand, man! There's a bottle of *mustard* in here!"

"George," Ed looked George straight in the eye and smiled. "I know."

George took a step back, fumbled with the bottle, and opened his mouth halfway.

"Uh-oh. You're not going to..."

Ed finished tying the bandanna on his head, rolled up his sleeves, and grabbed a cutting knife. It was one minute to three o'clock.

"I promised Willy I would go back and bake my pie. That's what I'm going to do," Ed said to George. "I'm going to bake my pie."

George saw a genuine smile come over Ed's face as he spoke. Ed seemed relaxed for the first time today. George still thought mustard pie wasn't a good idea, but he was happy that Ed was smiling again, and that was enough for George. He just nodded and put the mustard on the table.

And that was when the bell rang, and the battle of the pies began for the second and final time.

"Father! Just this once!"

Jeremy shouted into the cell phone. 휴대전화 "All I ask is... Father? Father!"

His father had hung up. 전화를 끊다 Jeremy threw the cell phone at the wall of the trailer.

"Damn it!"

He stood up, grabbed the counter, and shoved it over. 떠밀다 All the supplies on the table crashed to the floor. A few people in the audience noticed this and jumped in alarm.

"Boss? What happened? Boss!?" Jeremy's assistant cried out in surprise.

Jeremy ignored him and jumped down from the trailer. He meant to just walk straight out of the main tent. 의도하다 He was sick and tired of being himself, Jeremy Lightfoot Jr., son of the millionaire. 백만장자 He was just one step away from the back door when a voice called out to him.

"Jeremy!"

Jeremy stopped with his hands on the door. The voice came from the stands above him.

"Jeremy! Don't go! Jeremy!"

The voice cried out again. A very young voice. *Voices*, actually — because now his name was shouted from all over the stands above. Jeremy quietly looked up.

"Jeremy! You're the greatest!"

"Jeremy! Are you okay? Jeremy!"

Twenty or thirty children were crammed overhead in the
stands, cheering and shouting. They had realized something was
wrong, and had gathered above the Zombie Pies trailer. One of
them started singing the Zombie Pies song and they all joined in.

" ♪ *In the middle of the night, it's a heck of a fright! 'Cause the
Zombie's in the kitchen and your stomach is all itchin.' So get out of that
door, make your life a roar... Go to Zombie Pies! Go to Zombie Pies!* ♪ "

Jeremy lowered his eyes, but the singing continued. He stayed
that way, waiting for them to stop, but they kept on singing and
singing.

"Ahhh, you meddling brats!" Jeremy still had his head down,
but he spoke in a low, fiendish voice. When he raised his head, he
had a pair of fake Dracula teeth in his mouth.

"You dare speak that way to the Zombie Lord!? The Zombie Lord is always triumphant!"

The kids cheered in delight. Jeremy gave a monster-like laugh and walked back up the stairs into the trailer. Once he was safely inside, he threw away the fake teeth and grabbed an apron. He shouted to his assistant.

"Forget everything. We're going to Plan B. I'm doing *Inferno*."

"Sir!?" Now the assistant was really upset. "But that pie is dangerous! You nearly burned yourself to death when you tried it in the lab!"

"I don't care. Get the marshmallows ready," Jeremy shouted as he spread flour on the surface of his counter. "I'll get the blowtorch from the truck."

But before he got started, Jeremy took a glance towards Ed, and then over at Billy Bob, who stood behind the trailer. Maybe he couldn't win at his father's game, but he still had his own way of playing.

And the game wasn't over yet.

"Okay, pie-lovers! I'm Robert R. Silverman! We're back again for the relaunch of the PIEGAMES!" The television broadcast has already ended, so you folks here will be the only witnesses to the outcome today.

"It's five minutes past three and we're back on track with the rematch of the PIEGAMES!" Two crowd favorites, Zombie Pies and Brown Butters are off to a quick start. Zombie Pies looks especially busy. They're using a giant mixer to beat something up.

"Meanwhile, across the stadium from Zombie Pies you'll find Ed Wishbone and his faithful partner 'the Tux'! Too bad they weren't able to complete their pies this morning."

"Well, what's this? Mr. Wishbone seems to have changed his recipe this time... and... oh my God, Ed! What the hell are you doing!?"

Ed poured a bottle of mustard into a hot saucepan right in front of the host. The mustard instantly bubbled and a sharp smell rose into the air.

"I'm sorry to tell you this, Ed, but I think you've made a terrible mistake." The host spoke to Ed with a sour face. "Oh man, *that* is not blueberry. It isn't even blue!"

Half of the audience laughed. The other half frowned as they smelled the burning odor of mustard. Ed ignored the banter and stayed focused on his saucepan. He grabbed a bottle of lemon juice and mixed in several spoonfuls of the liquid. The host seemed a bit irritated that Ed was not listening to him.

"Oh man, Ed! A *mustard* pie? I feel sorry for the judges."

Ed kept working. With quick movements, he added half a cup of honey, a few spices, and a bag of cottage cheese to the pan. Then he tossed in a big bowl of graham crackers that George had crushed, and stirred the entire mixture with a large wooden spoon.

"Uhhm... that looks almost like food if you..." That was the moment a rich spicy aroma rose up out of the saucepan and reached the host's nose. The host's high-speed patter slowed down for the first time today as he inhaled the sweet and sour smell of Ed's recipe.

Some of the laughter from the audience also died down. They finally noticed the serious, determined look on Ed's face. Ed threw a splash of red wine into the pan. The wine caught fire and burned high for a moment. The mouth-watering smell grew even richer in the air. Suddenly, the barrel oven, the mustard, and the tuxedo weren't as funny as before.

"George! The crust!" Ed shouted to George as the audience watched.

George dashed to the oven. He took out a beautiful golden-brown crust from inside. It too gave off a slight smell of mustard. Spicy, but sweet. The host cleared his throat and spoke in a somewhat lowered tone.

"Well, okay. Let's see how the other contestants are doing. Here in the next booth, we have the famous Buffi Brothers..."

The host started walking away to the next booth, but couldn't help glancing back at Ed. The smell was growing richer and richer, filling the whole stadium now.

"George! How are the pies?"

"Looking good! Give them another five minutes."

"Gotcha," Ed said, and George smiled.

"Anything else?" George asked.

"Nope. Now we wait."

It had been a fast, yet incredibly long, hour and a half. Ed was finally able to relax and take a deep breath. That was when he saw something walk past the back door. It made him freeze.

"Cat?" Ed rubbed his eyes. "No. Can't be..."

Ed walked slowly to the back door and peered down the alley. There was no sign of anything. He was half convinced it had just been his imagination. But a number of boxes and crates were lined up along the wall, and there were plenty of hiding spaces for a cat.

"Ed, where you goin'?" George asked with a worried look as Ed took a step out the back door.

"Nowhere... Just getting some fresh air," he answered.

"Come back soon, man! The pie's almost finished."

"Sure," Ed replied, but he was focused on movement in the back alley.

"Cat... You're not there, are you? Cat?"

Ed whispered as he walked past a pile of boxes. Nothing was there but some trash. He reached the end of the alley and opened the emergency exit to look outside. There was only an empty field beyond it. He sighed with relief.

At that exact moment, Billy Bob stepped out from behind Ed and grabbed him by the neck. In a moment of panic, Ed tried to loosen Billy Bob's grip, but Billy Bob was much, much stronger.

"Give up. Quit the game. Now," Billy Bob whispered.

Ed kept clawing at Billy Bob's hands. But it was no use. He choked and gasped as Billy Bob tightened his grip further. Ed's face was starting to turn blue.

"Stop! Goddammit! Stop! You're going to kill him!"

Someone hit Billy Bob in the back with a gasoline can. Billy Bob grabbed the intruder and slammed him against the boxes near Ed. There was a mild expression of surprise on his face when he saw that it was his boss's son.

Jeremy scrambled to his knees and shouted at Billy Bob.

"You stop this right now or I'll call the police."

Billy Bob ignored Jeremy and turned to Ed again.

"I'm not going to quit," Ed said abruptly. His legs were shaking badly with fear, and he was almost in tears, but he went on anyway. "They're waiting for me back on Ghost Avenue. I can't quit."

Ed was trying really hard to stand up straight, but his thin, weak legs refused to hold him up. Billy Bob didn't hesitate. He moved towards Ed. Only moments before Billy Bob's hands reached Ed, a low purr came from the ground below.

All three looked down.

Mr. Jones had finally found its way back and was brushing its side against Jeremy's leg. It went over to Billy Bob and started rolling around on his shoes, purring all the while.

Billy Bob watched this through his dark sunglasses. The two pie bakers continued to huddle on the ground while the cat went on rolling. A long, awkward moment passed. Billy Bob shook his head.

"You," he said to Ed. "You need more spice."

Ed kept quiet, not knowing what to say. He was still recovering his breath. He didn't know whether Billy Bob was referring to him or his pie. Billy Bob turned to Jeremy.

"And you. It's Ms.! Not Mr.! Next time, *check*, you stupid brat!"

Having said that, Billy Bob took a long breath. He looked at the bewildered faces of the two, shook his head again, and walked off without another word. Ed and Jeremy stared at each other.

"What... what was that all about?" Jeremy murmured.

"I have no..."

Ed suddenly remembered the time and grabbed Jeremy's arm. He took a quick look at Jeremy's watch. He gasped, and hurried to his feet. Still shaking, he ran back to his booth on weak legs.

Left alone with Mr. Jones, Jeremy sat there for a while, mumbling something to himself. Then, suddenly — he understood what Billy Bob had said.

Jeremy grabbed Mr. Jones and raised the cat up in the air. Mr. Jones relaxed and purred.

A moment later, Jeremy's eyes opened wide with surprise.

Fifteen more minutes.

George had to make a choice.

The rims^{가장자리} of the pie were already a bit too brown. In a few
seconds, it would be too late. Ed had not come back and it was
up to him to rescue the pies.

He was scared to do anything, but he knew in his heart that
if he didn't get the pies out now, they would burn. So he took a
deep breath, prayed that he was doing what was right, and pulled
out the two pies.

As George was laying the two pies on the table, a wheezy^{헐떡거리는} Ed
came tumbling into the booth behind him.

"George, are the pies okay?"

"Ed! God! I was so worried, man! I didn't know what to
do!"

Ed looked at the pies on the table and sighed with relief.

"George. Thanks. You were great. Now, c'mon, let's finish.
We only have ten more minutes."

"Gotcha!" George replied and handed Ed the decorations ^{장식}
they had made from sugar and marzipan. _(호두, 달걀, 아몬드 등을 넣어 만든 과자) Ed was about to place
the first one on the pie when he suddenly stopped.

"Something wrong?" George asked.

"No," Ed said. "It's just..."

The pie was beautiful the way it was. It had only a simple
golden-yellow surface, but the color was beautiful. Ed hesitated.
He looked around the arena at the other booths.

Most of the pies were finished. They were all decorated with
splendid colors, looking more like works of art than food. The ^{다채로운}
whole arena was also much like the pies. All colorful, glamorous, ^{화려한}
and wonderful.

But as he stood there looking around, it all suddenly seemed
strange to Ed. For a few seconds, all of the sound and racket ^{떠드는 소리}

faded into the distance, and Ed could see for the first time —
without any distraction — the whole scene of the contest before
him. And it seemed strange. It seemed like he was lost in a world
he didn't know.

He remembered his mother's pie. So simple, so beautiful.

He remembered the fake apple pie he had made that first
morning on Ghost Avenue. It was simple too. Maybe not
beautiful, but simple and warm.

Ed quietly put the decorations back down. He said to George,
"Let's leave it this way."

George gasped.

"Why?! Ed! Are you out of your mind? Look at all the other
pies, man!"

Ed smiled. "This is our pie. It has to be simple."

George was dumbfounded for a moment, but he looked at the decorations, then at Ed, then at the barrel oven, and then finally, at himself.

"I... I guess you're right," George said. "There ain't no decorations on Ghost Avenue, you know."

That made them both smile. Ed added a simple ring of yellow whipped cream around the rims of the pies, then handed the two pies to George. George went running to the judges' booth.

Jeremy walked out of the Zombie Pies trailer almost at the same time. His assistant was rolling a giant carrier. Ed and Jeremy's eyes met across the arena.

A few minutes later, the bell rang for the second time, and the PIEGAMES were officially over.

"Good evening! This is Glen Hamperton reporting for the evening news. We're back at the state pie festival! Hundreds have called us insisting that we follow up on the rematch of the contest... Well, here we are with a special live report, just in time for the finale."

"The baking is all finished. The contestants are now presenting their pies to the audience. The local Chinese favorite, 'Sugar & Spice,' has just finished their mystic oriental dragon dance... and now Goo Goo Planet is up on stage. Something like a flying saucer is landing in the middle of the stage."

"Uhm... too bad. The audience doesn't like them too much. Frankly, I don't blame them. Thank God... it seems to be over now."

"Only a few contestants seem to be left, and... oh-oh, a weird drum beat has just started up in the arena... Is that..."

"Yes! It is! Ladies and gentlemen, you're all in luck, because we're just in time for the big show! Here they come! Get ready!"

"*ZOMBIE PIES!!*"

A cloud of red smoke began to fill the arena as a low beating of drums sounded inside the tent. The smoke suddenly parted in the middle, and Jeremy appeared from within the cloud.

The Gravedigger followed behind him, carrying a huge tray with a blue velvet cloth spread over it. Red spotlights from the top of the Zombie Pies trailer flew around Jeremy as the volume of the music stepped up.

"Behold!! The fiery gates of the Inferno!" Jeremy shouted and drew the velvet cloth from the tray. A huge pie that resembled a red forest in a snow-covered land appeared from under the cloth.

Jeremy raised his hand and the music suddenly stopped. The Gravedigger placed the tray on a stand and hurried away.

The audience fell silent, staring at Jeremy and his pie. After standing absolutely^완전히 still for a moment, Jeremy waved his hand at the pie. A giant blaze^불길 of fire burst out from under his cape. It covered the surface of the pie in flames^화염 for a few seconds, then disappeared as suddenly as it had appeared. After the fire, the soft, marshmallow-white surface of the pie had been toasted a delicious golden-brown. The forest had melted into a spectacular^볼 만한 mound^작은 산 of red toffee.^토피(설탕, 버터 등으로 만든 과자)

The crowd applauded intensely^열렬히 as Jeremy took a bow.^인사

Meanwhile, behind the stage.

"Ed. You all right, man?"

"I don't know."

"You're up next."

Ed nodded. George looked around the stands surrounding them, and said in a weak voice.

"Man, I'd be scared if I was you."

"George, I *am* scared," Ed assured him.

"Ed Wishbone, will you please come to the stage!" The voice from the speakers called his name.

"That's you," George said.

Ed just nodded again and started walking towards the stage. His legs were stiff as sticks. On the last moment, George remembered to hand Ed something. Ed took it and opened his hand. Willy's fortune cookie lay in his palm. Ed took a deep breath, and managed a smile.

"Thanks, George. I'll try my best."

Jeremy was just coming down from the stage. Ed and Jeremy's eyes met as they passed each other.

"Your turn," Jeremy said. It was only a whisper. He was holding his right hand inside his cape. Ed noticed it was burned pretty badly. Jeremy's assistant came rushing up to him with a bucket of ice water as soon as Jeremy sat down. Jeremy dipped his hand in the bucket and grunted with pain.

"Ed Wishbone? Are you there?"

The announcer called out again. Ed walked out onto the stage. A spotlight came searching for him.

As the spotlight guided him to the center of the stage, Ed was surprised to hear a lot of clapping coming from the audience. He saw a microphone waiting for him. His pies were there too, displayed on a table. He walked forward, but very stiffly.

When he reached the microphone, Ed took a breath and looked around the arena. Hundreds, maybe thousands of eyes fell on him. He swallowed.

He tried to say something, but his mind was completely blank. He tried to think of something to say, anything, but his brain simply refused to work.

"Hello."

He said finally, his voice trembling a little. A few people in the audience laughed.

"I'm Ed Wishbone. I used to own a pie shop. But now, I live down on Ghost Avenue."

A stir went through the crowd.

"A lot of people live there — and they're all kind to me. They... they are poor. Really poor. It's certainly not the best place to live, but it's... it's still my home. It's the only home I have."

As he spoke, Ed felt the warmth of the campfire in the cinema. The peaceful night sky above Ghost Avenue spread through him. He opened his hands and was surprised that the sweat on his palms had dried. He felt a little calmer than before.

"These past weeks have been a very hard time for me... But somehow, it all seems a lot more precious than the rest of my life. Weeks that I'll never forget."

A quiet rush of memories flew through Ed's mind as he said these words. Losing his shop, running to the bank, waking up in a ghost town... everything seemed like such a long time ago. Ed took a long, deep breath, and continued.

"Sometimes... I think the best pie isn't always sweet. Sometimes it's not sour or bitter either. Sometimes... I think... I think that it can even be a mustard pie."

Ed lowered his eyes to his pie. And for a second, the words Billy Bob had said to him came back as an echo.

Spice. You need more spice.

"It's a little spicy at first, but we all need some spice to recognize the sweetness hidden underneath. I've learned in these past few weeks that a good pie is a lot like real life. Everyone's life.

I used to spend a lot of time leaning on the counter of my old pie shop, wondering why no one came to buy my pies. But I think I know now."

The audience had become almost completely silent. Ed was so absorbed in his thoughts that he didn't notice.

"I tried so hard to make good pies... great pies, but being a baker, a pie baker, isn't really about making pies..." Ed took another deep breath, and said in a firm voice, "it's about making people happy."

The audience remained silent. Ed had expected laughter, so he felt relieved as he whispered into the microphone.

"Uh... That's all. Thank you for listening. Thank you."

The applause that came a moment later was big. Really big. And the applause continued — for a long, long time.

The cat walked down the center of the fairgrounds gracefully,
almost dragging its full tummy on the ground. It suddenly came
to a stop when Ed stepped out of the main tent, his bandanna in
one hand and an exhausted look on his face. Ed spotted the cat
immediately, but didn't seem surprised.

"I thought I saw you," Ed said to the cat.
The cat cautiously retreated a few steps.

"Don't worry, the contest's almost over. I'm not going to try
and catch you and get my only good shirt ripped."

Ed sat down on a bench near the cat. The cat frowned, but
decided Ed was not a concern.

Ed watched the glimmering lights of the carnival in silence,
with the cat at his feet. The applause was still echoing back
inside the arena, but it all seemed far away. The glamour, the
importance, and the meaning of the contest felt vague to Ed as he
sat there.

Ed looked at the cat. Their eyes met for a moment.

"I used to have a fairly peaceful life, you know," Ed said softly. "Until that day you came into my shop. Since then, my life has been one big roller-coaster ride. No thanks to you."

The cat seemed not to care. It just yawned and continued licking its paws.

"But you know what, cat?" Ed said. "I think I'm starting to like roller coasters."

A low purr echoed a few feet away. Ed looked up. He saw Jeremy sneaking out of the tent with a cat cage in one hand. Jeremy had his heavy coat on, and seemed to be leaving.

"Damn," Jeremy said. "Why are you out here?"

Ed shrugged. "What about you?"

Jeremy's cat purred again in its cage. The Big Fat Cat opened one eye, took a look, and then closed it.

"I'm going home," Jeremy said.

"Why? What about the results?"

Jeremy sighed.

"I'm smart enough to know when I've lost. I just don't want to see the kids when they find out. And your pie..."

Jeremy realized he was talking too much. He coughed, and went on more slowly.

"...Uh, nothing. Well, anyway, it's okay. I really don't need the prize money, you know." He shrugged. "I'm rich."

"Ed!"

Just then, George flew out of the main tent, a look of awe [두려움] on his face. He was trying to say something, but the words seemed to be stuck [달라붙다] in his mouth.

"George." Ed rose [일어나다], worried that something had happened again. "Is everything okay? Did the judges reach a decision [결정]?"

George smiled, and with tears forming [고이다] in his eyes, said in a warm voice.

"Oh yeah. Yeah, they sure did."

Jeremy shrugged as he watched Ed and George run back into the main tent, back into the growing applause. He said to The Cat Formerly [이전에] Known As Mr. Jones,

"Don't worry. I'm okay." Jeremy patted [가볍게 두드리다] the cat's cage. "C'mon, let's go home."

Jeremy slowly walked away into the night, whistling the theme music of Zombie Pies.

"Willy! BeeJees! Frank! We're back! We've got the money!"

Ed called out as he entered the cinema. George was one step behind him. The cinema lobby was almost completely dark. Ed and George hurried through the piles of junk.

"C'mon! There's a taxi waiting outside! I already called the hospital!"

Ed shouted louder as he approached the swinging doors.

"I'm sorry I'm late! We had an accident and..."

Ed pushed the doors open and stopped short. The hall was silent. His voice echoed in the empty space.

"Willy?"

The cinema was absolutely silent. Step by step, Ed slowly approached Willy.

Willy was completely still. Not only Willy, but the air around him also seemed still. Time itself seemed still there. Ed knew that Willy was dead.

"It was about an hour ago," BeeJees said. He held his face in his hands, squatting against the ragged bed.

"He suddenly opened his eyes and smiled. I thought maybe he was waking up and I ran over to him. He was already dead."

"Wh... why..."

But Ed couldn't continue. The words remained in his mouth. He tried to swallow, but his mouth was dry. Willy wore a smile on his face. He looked like he was proud of something.

"I think he knew," BeeJees said as he laid his eyes on the
트로피
trophy in Ed's hands. Tears gleamed in his eyes. "I think he
반짝이다
knew."

Ed closed his eyes tight. He was trembling slightly.
꽉

The light of the moon was a soft tender yellow against the
부드러운
darkness of the world. It shined on Willy as if it were guiding
him to a better world. A world without hunger or pain or cold.
배고픔
A world where he could finally rest. A world that was not cruel
잔인한
like the one they had to live in.

"I don't know how... But I..." BeeJees broke down as he spoke.
"I... really think he knew... and I think... I think he was happy."

The Golden Crust trophy glittered in the moonlight as it fell
반짝이다
from Ed's hands, rolled on the floor, and lay still in the dark.

The silence of the night slowly eased the tension of the long hard day. The temperature was almost below zero. Ed's breath turned white as he walked down the dark street, the Golden Crust trophy in his hands. He chose a place on the sidewalk, and sat looking up at the stars. He watched them for a long time, as if he could find Willy among them — if he looked hard enough.

Behind Ed, the cat played around with the Golden Crust trophy. The cat had realized it wasn't a real pie some time ago, but it kept playing anyway.

All the excitement of the day seemed like a dream far away as Ed sat there in the cold. He remembered the day he met Willy, right there on the street. He remembered his soft voice. He remembered his careful words. And most of all, he remembered his soothing smile.

"What am I going to do now, Willy?" Ed whispered into the empty space around him. The words turned white and disappeared immediately. "What, Willy? *What?*"

After a long pause, Ed took the fortune cookie out of his pocket. He stared at it for a moment, then cracked it open. A thin piece of paper was inside. Ed read it.

Most treasures are in the places you first find them.

Ed read it over and over again, trying to find some meaning in the words. Some answer. But only tears came and fell. He cuddled his knees and cried. The cat just continued to play with the trophy.

Up above town, the first flakes of snow started to fall,
announcing the arrival of a long, cold season. A church bell rang
far away in the mountains. The snow quickly grew stronger, and
soon, the town of Everville was covered with the color of winter.

December 25th.
It was Christmas Day.

NEXT: One last story.

BFC BOOKS PRESENTS:
영어원서의 세계에서 길 찾기

슬슬 원서의 세계로 여행을 떠날 때.
배낭에 넣을 건 단 하나, 상상력뿐.
BFC이 드리는 초급자를 위한 영어원서 가이드.

PROLOGUE
~ 책을 찾아 떠나는 여행 ~

여러분의 성원에 힘입어 장장 6권까지 이어진 Big Fat Cat 시리즈도 어느새 한 권만 남았습니다. 고양이와 에드의 여행이 끝나는 종착역도 어딘지 이제 곧 알 수 있겠지요. Big Fat Cat 시리즈는 이 시점에서 하나의 결말을 맞이하겠지만, 영어의 묘미를 깨칠 수 있는 여행은 계속됩니다.

이 세상에는 재미있는 책이 참으로 많이 있습니다. Big Fat Cat 시리즈를 지금까지 읽어온 분이라면(건너뛰고 읽은 분이라도 괜찮습니다) 이미 세상에 나와 있는 영어소설을 읽을 준비는 마친 셈입니다. 아직 영어소설을 읽어보지 못했다면 슬슬 드넓은 원서의 세계로 들어설 때입니다.

하지만 어떤 책을 읽으면 좋을지 잘 모르거나 읽고 싶은 책을 찾지 못한 분도 있겠지요. 그런 분들께는 영어로 된 어린이 도서를 꼭 읽어보라고 권하고 싶습니다.

결코 간단해서가 아닙니다. 어른 대상의 책에 비해 확실히 읽기는 쉽지만 이는 부차적인 이유에 불과합니다. 어린이 책을 권하는 이유는 어린이 책이야말로 가장 재미있는 책의 장르이기 때문입니다.

미국의 평범한 집에는 대개 책꽂이에 많은 어린이 책들이 꽂혀 있습니다. 아이만을 위해서가 아닙니다. 어른 한 권씩 소중히 꽂아둡니다. 왜 이처럼 어른 아이 할 것 없이 어린이 도서를 좋아하는지 우선 그 비밀을 밝혀보기로 하지요. 빅팻캣 시리즈의 마지막 해설에서는 천천히 여러분을 '어린이 책의 세계'로 안내하고자 합니다.

Jeremy Lightfoot Jr.'s
Words *of* **Wisdom**

"Time is money.
But the exchange rate is low."

Jerry Lightfoot Jr.

책과 함께 크는 아이들

미국은 어린이 책의 천국과 같은 곳입니다.

어른도 푹 빠져서 페이지를 넘길 만한 재미있는 이야기부터 미술관에 진열할 만큼 멋진 그림책까지 훌륭한 책이 많이 있습니다. 또한 알록달록 다채롭게 꾸며진 어린이 도서관(Children's Library)이 어느 마을에나 있어서 마음껏 책을 빌려볼 수 있어요. 물론 어린이 도서관에는 영상자료나 오디오북도 풍부하지요. 뿐만 아니라 계절마다 '독서 그랑프리'가 열려서 아이들이 한 달 동안 읽은 책의 권수를 가지고 서로 경쟁합니다. 대회에서 우승하면 멋진 상품을 받게 되므로 아이들도 열성적으로 참여해요. 우승한 아이는 한 달에 100권 이상 책을 읽기도 하는데 이는 결코 드문 일이 아닙니다.

의외로 잘 알려져 있지 않지만, 미국은 교육과정에서 '독서'를 매우 중시합니다. 초등학교마다 대부분 알찬 도서실(규모가 큰 학교는 도서관)을 갖추고 있고, 과제에 따라서는 '도서실에 가서 조사할 것'이라고 조건을 달기 때문에 모르는 것이 생기면 도서관에 가는 습관이 몸에 배어 있어요.

독서과제도 종종 주어집니다. 그러나 무턱대고 '읽으라'고 강요하지는 않습니다. 화려한 일러스트로 꾸며진 책을 선별해서 도서목록을 나눠주고, 아이 스스로 마음에 드는 책을 고르도록 유도하지요. 도서목록도 꼭 '명작'이나 '양서'라고 할 만한 작품만 뽑지는 않고 '아이 눈높이에서 볼 때 정말 재미있는 책'을 중심으로 선별해요.

처음에 읽은 책이 재미없으면 그 아이는 일생 동안 책과 멀어질 수도 있습니다. 그러므로 어린이 권장도서목록을 만들 때면 매우 진지하고 신중하게 한 권 한 권 정성껏 고르지요. 이런 정성 덕분에 도서목록에 있는 어떤 책을 선택해도 아이들은 책과 함께하는 마법의 시간을 맛볼 수 있답니다.

아래 만화에 고집불통 소년이 등장하네요. 이 소년의 초등학교 시절 독서체험을 통해서 미국인들이 책을 좋아하게 되는 과정을 함께 감상해보세요.

①선생님에게서 권장도서목록을 받는다

②마지못해 표지가 근사한 책을 고른다

③한참 동안 거들떠보지도 않는다

④심심한 참에 점심시간에 몇 페이지만 읽어본다

⑤왠지 그 다음이 궁금해진다

⑥하교길에 체육관 뒤편 계단에 쭈그리고 앉아 읽기 시작한다

⑦계속 읽는다

⑧계속 읽는다

⑨끝까지 읽는다(귀가시간이 늦어져서 꾸중을 듣는다)

⑩팔랑팔랑 책장을 넘기며 다시 들추어 본다

⑪뭔가 읽을거리가 없으면 심심하다

⑫이하 상상에 맡긴다

⑬그리고…… 30년 후

⑭역사는 반복된다

⑮앞으로도 계속……

미국인 대부분이 이런 과정을 거치며 책을 좋아하게 됩니다. 한 권의 소설책을 닳도록 읽고 난 다음 영화로 만들어지면 제일 앞줄에서 봅니다. 그리고 자라서 자신이 부모가 되면 그 책을 아이에게 사줍니다. 새로운 판이 출간되어 표지가 바뀐 그 책을 아이보다 먼저 읽고는 '역시 재밌어!'라고 말하면서요.

Not so long ago...

안타깝게도 아직 우리나라는 미국만큼 독서를 중시하는 환경을 갖추지 못했습니다. 아이들은 어린이 도서보다 만화에 열중해요. 만화가 더 재미있으니 무리도 아니지요. 미국의 아이들이 어린이 책을 읽는 이유는 단순해요. 어린이 책들이 만화 못지않게 재미있기 때문입니다.

책을 가까이 하며 자란 사람들은 대부분 어른이 되어서도 어린이 도서를 즐겨 읽습니다. 좋아하는 시리즈가 발간될 때마다 몇십 년에 걸쳐 꾸준히 사는 사람도 적지 않지요. 그 이유는 어린이 도서가 일반도서의 하위 장르로 치부되지 않고, 실제로 일반도서 버금가는, 때로는 그 이상으로 훌륭한 어린이 도서가 많기 때문입니다. 또한 재미의 측면에서도 어른용과 아이용으로 굳이 구분하지 않아요.

그래서 어른이 된 후 자신만의 '베스트 100권'을 꼽으라고 하면, 책을 좋아하는 미국인의 목록에는 흔히 어린이 도서가 몇 권 포함돼요. 이는 일반서적을 수없이 많이 읽은 후에도 어린이 도서의 작품성이 빛을 바래지 않기 때문입니다. 만약 여러분도 이런 한 권의 책을 만나게 된다면 한결 영어가 좋아지지 않을까요.

물론 수많은 어린이 도서들 중에서 좋은 책을 찾기란 쉬운 일이 아닙니다. 게다가 영어가 모국어가 아닌 사람이 마음에 맞는 책을 찾으려면 영어의 '난이도'와 '재미'가 균형을 이루어야 하므로 매우 어려운 과제가 돼요. 예외가 있기는 하지만 대개 난이도가 올라갈수록 표현력도 좋아지므로 어느 정도 난이도가 있는 책이 역시 깊이 있고 치밀한 이야기일 가능성이 높지요. 다만 그렇다고 해서 처음부터 난이도가 높은 책에 도전했다가는 '재미'를 느끼기도 전에 지쳐버리기 십상입니다.

자신의 수준에 적합한 난이도는 '사전을 거의 펼쳐보지 않고도 조바심내지 않고 읽을 수 있는 책'입니다. 하지만 충분히 이해가 간다 해도 재미가 없다면 역시 끝까지 읽지 못하게 돼요. 이처럼 즐겁게 읽을 수 있는 수준 내에서 가장 재미있는 책을 발견하기란 결코 쉽지 않은 일이지요.

There was a box full of kittens
on the side of a road.

이번 해설에서는 이런 탐색을 위한 길잡이로 권장도서목록을 만들어보았습니다. 목록이라고 해도 처음에 소개할 책은 단 세 권뿐이에요. 즉 '기본 세 권'이 되는 작품들입니다. 세 작품 모두 〈Big Fat Cat and the Fortune Cookie〉와 비슷한 난이도이며, 분위기나 내용도 빅팻캣 시리즈와 비슷한 느낌이에요. 내용을 이해하는 데 도움이 되는 삽화도 많이 삽입되어 있습니다.

우선 이 '기본 세 권'을 통해서 영어원서의 세계에 발을 들여놓길 바랍니다.

Two were white, two were striped,
and two had spots on their back.

Please take me home

STEP 1
~ 책을 고른다 ~

'기본 세 권' 중에서 가장 먼저 소개하고자 하는 책은 온갖 신기한 과자로 페이지를 채운 걸작 판타지 〈Charlie and the Chocolate Factory〉입니다.

CHARLIE AND THE CHOCOLATE FACTORY

Charlie and the Chocolate Factory by Roald Dahl
이 이야기의 주인공 찰리는 병들어 누워 지내는 할아버지, 할머니와 함께 사는 가난한 소년입니다. 찰리는 초콜릿을 무척 좋아하지만 좀처럼 살 수 없어요. 하지만 찰리의 집 바로 옆에는 세계에서 가장 크고 유명한 '윌리 웡카 초콜릿 공장'이 있어서 늘 달콤한 초콜릿향이 풍겨오지요. 찰리는 단 한 번만이라도 좋으니 공장을 구경하고 싶어해요.

그러던 어느 날 공장을 견학할 수 있는 '골든 티켓'이 초콜릿 바의 포장지 속에 들어 있다는 뉴스가 흘러나오지요. 마을은 온통 들썩이고 다들 초콜릿을 사려고 혈안이 되지만, 찰리가 얻은 초콜릿은 생일날 받은 딱 한 개뿐입니다. 더구나 골든 티켓은 전 세계를 통틀어 겨우 다섯 장. 과연 찰리의 초콜릿 속에는……?

And one was a dark color.

Please take me home

두 번째 추천작품은 학생과 선생님 간에 밀고 당기는 유머러스한 전쟁이 그려진, 신선한 코미디 〈Frindle〉입니다. 예측불허로 전개되는 이야기와 감동적인 마지막 장면이 언제까지나 마음에 남는 작품이에요.

Frindle by Andrew Clements

닉 앨런은 학교수업을 방해하는 천재소년입니다. 아무리 지루한 수업이라도 닉이 관련되면 아이들 바람대로 흥미진진해져요. 이처럼 똑똑한 말썽꾸러기인 닉은 새 학년이 되자 학교에서 가장 엄하기로 소문난 그레인저 선생님 반으로 배정을 받습니다. 닉은 반 친구들의 기대를 등에 업고 '훼방꾼'이라는 명성에 걸맞게 그레인저 선생님이 숙제를 내주려는 순간 어려운 질문을 해서 숙제 내줄 시간을 없애려고 해요. 그러나 이런 수법은 전혀 통하지 않고 처음으로 패배를 맛보지요.

이대로 물러설 수 없었던 닉은 어느 날 수업시간에 그레인저 선생님이 '언어는 누구나 발명할 수 있는 것'이라고 하자 이를 계기로 볼펜을 '프린들'이라고 부르기 시작합니다. 사전을 숭배하는 국어교사 그레인저 선생님은 닉을 엄하게 꾸짖지만, 어느새 반 아이들 전원이 볼펜을 '프린들'이라고 부르기 시작하고 차차 마을 전체로 퍼져서 급기야 TV 방송국에서 찾아오는 소동이 벌어집니다. 결국 닉이 상상조차 못했던 사태가……

마지막으로 세 번째 작품은 가끔씩 엉뚱하기 짝이 없는 한 천재소녀를 둘러싼 이야기입니다. 불쑥불쑥 등장하는 뜻밖의 장면과 서정적인 분위기가 묘한 균형을 이루며 이야기가 펼쳐져요. 독자를 울리고 웃기는 작품 중의 하나입니다.

They all meowed and meowed at passing strangers — all except for the dark kitten.

Please take me home

Someday Angeline *by Louis Sachar*

앤절린은 모르는 것이 없는 여덟 살배기 천재소녀입니다. 하지만 바로 이 때문에 주변의 모든 사람들에게서 왕따를 당합니다. 쓰레기 트럭을 모는 앤절린의 아버지는 우둔한 자신에게서 어떻게 이런 딸이 태어났는지 알지 못한 채, 자신의 존재가 앤절린의 장래를 망치지는 않을까 하는 두려움에 점차 딸과 거리를 둡니다. 앤절린이 품고 있는 단 한 가지 소원은 아버지와 평범하고 행복하게 살아가는 것. 하지만 앤절린의 천재적인 머리도 그 소원만큼은 어떻게 해야 하는지 방법을 알 수 없어요. 그런 앤절린에게 처음으로 생긴 친구가 떠벌이 군. 늘 시시덕거리기만 하는 군은 반 친구들 모두에게서 무시를 당하고 매사에 뒤처지는 소년. 하지만 군은 앤절린이 천재라는 사실을 전혀 개의치 않았습니다. 이윽고 앤절린을 이해해주는 선생님도 나타나고 모든 것이 술술 풀린다고 생각할 무렵 운명의 바퀴가 멋대로 굴러가기 시작하는데요……

세 권의 줄거리를 읽고 나니 마음에 드는 책이 있나요? 어느 책이나 결코 간단하지는 않지만 문장 자체는 읽기 쉽고 이야기나 등장인물도 친근한 작품들입니다. 우선 이 중에서 한 권을 골라보세요. 줄거리만으로는 도저히 못 고르겠다는 분은 다음 차트로!

They were all hungry,
so they cried and cried.

Please take me home

'기본 세 권'을 선택하기 위한 **Help Chart**

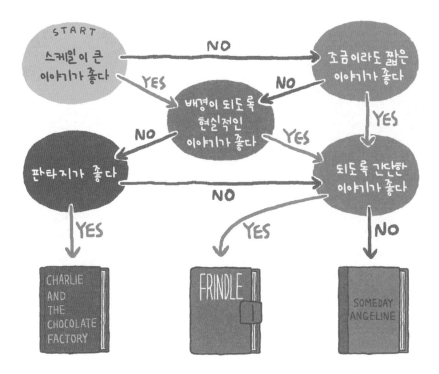

일반 영어원서에는 Big Fat Cat 시리즈처럼 뜻풀이는 물론 3색사진도 없습니다. 줄거리를 읽었지만 '과연 내가 읽을 수 있을까' 하고 불안을 느끼는 분도 많이 있으리라고 생각해요. 긴장하면 충분히 이해할 수 있는 내용도 잘 이해가 되지 않으므로 그럴 때는 무리하지 말고 더쉬운 책을 골라보세요.

예를 들면 이런 책은 어떨까요?

Marvin Redpost: Kidnapped at Birth?
by Louis Sachar

마빈 레드포스트는 어디서나 흔히 볼 수 있는 남자 아이로 초등학생입니다. 어느 날 신문에서 샴푼나라(Shampoon)의 왕이 어릴 때 유괴된 자신의 아이를 찾고 있다는 기사를 읽고 강한 의혹을 품어요. 기사에 나온 아이의 특징이 자신과 너무 닮았기 때문이지요.

하지만 자신이 왕의 아이일 리는 없고……. 마빈은 머리로는 그럴 리 없다고 생각하면서도 신경이 쓰여서 가만히 있을 수가 없습니다. 의혹은 점점 깊어만 가고 마빈은 엉뚱한 행동을…….

이 책은 '기본 세 권' 중의 하나로 소개한 〈Someday Angeline〉의 작가가 쓴 가벼운 코미디입니다. 문장은 〈Big Fat Cat and the Mustard Pie〉와 비슷한 난이도로, 약간 어려운 단어도 나오지만 까다로운 표현이나 관용구는 나오지 않아요.

기본 세 권이나 더 쉬운 한 권 중 어느 책이나 좋습니다. 한 권을 골랐다면 다음 페이지로 넘어가세요.

The kittens left in the box meowed sadly, except the dark one that just yawned.

Please take me home

STEP 2
~책을 손에 넣는다~

자, 읽고 싶은 책은 정해졌지요? 이제 이 책을 어디서 구해야 할까요?

영어원서를 구하는 방법은 크게 네 가지입니다. 우선 근처의 도서관으로 가봅니다. 꼭 영어 도서관이 아니더라도 요즘은 일반 도서관에도 영어책을 많이 비치해놓았으므로 가서 찾아보면 BIG FAT CAT이 추천하는 원서들 다수는 찾을 수 있답니다. 앞 페이지들을 들춰보며 내가 읽을 수 있는 레벨의 문장들인지 체크해보는 것도 좋은 습관입니다. 만약 안타깝게도 도서관에 책이 없다면 사서 선생님들께 제목을 말씀드리고 책을 구해달라고 얘기해보세요. 얼마 지나지 않아 그 책을 구해주실 거예요.

도서관에서 빌려보기보다 아예 구입하고 싶다면 주변의 서점이나 인터넷 서점에서 찾아봅니다. 규모가 큰 서점에 가면 영어책 코너가 따로 있으므로 그곳에서 책을 찾아봅니다. 영어원서만을 모아서 판매하는 영어책 전문 서점도 있는데요, 이곳에 가면 대부분의 잘 알려진 어린이 영어책들은 바로 구입할 수 있습니다. 또한 인터넷 서점에서는 제목만 알면 대부분의 책을 검색할 수 있으므로 손쉽게 영어책을 구할 수 있어요. 인터넷 서점에서 책을 찾을 때는 같은 작가의 다른 책도 한꺼번에 찾아볼 수 있으므로 책에 대한 더 많은 정보를 얻을 수 있고 책 내용과 관련하여 다른 사람들이 써놓은 리뷰도 읽어보면 책을 선택하는 데 도움이 될 거예요.

우리나라에서 구할 수 없는 책은 해외 서점을 이용합니다. 해외 서점으로 가장 인기 있는 곳은 아마존이라는 인터넷 서점이 있어요. 인터넷으로 책을 검색하여 주문하면 어느 곳이라도 책을 보내줍니다. 우리나라에서 구입하는 것보다 저렴하게 살 수도 있지만, 배송비가 많이 들고 배송 시간이 오래 걸릴 수도 있으니 염두에 두세요. 해외 서점에서 책을 찾고 주문하는 과

One of the spotted kittens was weak.
It could only purr.
Everyone thought it was sick,
so they never picked it.

Please take me home

정이 다소 번거로울 수 있지만 한번만 해보면 그리 어렵지 않다는 것을 알게 될 거예요. 책 가격 자체도 우리나라와 비교해서 크게 차이가 나지 않으니 크게 부담 갖지 말고 해외도서 직접 구입을 경험해보는 것도 괜찮습니다.

마지막으로 여러분은 e-book으로 책을 읽어본 적이 있나요? 전자기기를 가지고 있다면 절차가 간편한 전자책으로 구입하여 읽어보는 것도 방법입니다. 아마존에서는 이미 많은 영어책들이 전자책 버전으로 나와서 판매하고 있답니다. 처음에는 종이로 된 책을 읽기만 해서인지 어색할 수도 있지만 내용은 똑같고 비용은 훨씬 저렴한 데다 배송 절차가 생략되어 있으니 신속하게 받아서 읽을 수 있다는 장점이 있어요.

원서라고 해서 구하는 방법이 어렵지는 않지요? 처음 영어원서를 주문하려면 이런저런 절차가 까다롭게 생각될 수도 있지만 그 절차가 영어 공부에 방해가 되진 않을 거예요. 오히려 영어와 가까워지는 첫걸음이 되기도 하지요. 서둘러 책을 주문하려 하면 귀찮은 절차가 되어버리지만 기다림을 영어를 배우는 즐거움의 하나로 여기고 여유롭게 주문해보세요. 책이 도착하기까지 시간이 짧게는 일주일, 길게는 20일 정도를 기다려야 하는 경우도 생길 거예요. 하지만 그렇게 구하기 힘든 영어책을 고르고 기다리고 도착해서 읽어보는 과정 자체가 책과 연관된 하나의 추억이 되기도 해요. 추억이 많은 책은 마음에 오래도록 남지요. 그러니 초조해하지 말고 천천히 즐기는 마음으로 추억을 쌓아가세요.

A man took the other spotted kitten. And now there were only two.

Please take me home

STEP 3
~ 책을 읽는다 ~

　사람마다 주문하는 방법은 다르겠지만, 앞의 방법대로 하면 드디어 한 권의 책을 받아볼 수 있습니다. 우리나라에서는 한 권의 책을 두 가지로 나누어 판매하는 일이 흔치 않지만 외국에서는 초기에는 하드커버로 판매하다가 나중에는 페이퍼백으로 만들어 판매하는 일이 많습니다. 페이퍼백은 책의 형태나 크기가 확실히 정해져 있지 않기 때문에, 재치가 번뜩이는 디자인도 많이 있지요. 값도 하드커버보다 저렴하고, 들고 다니기 좋도록 매우 가볍고 튼튼한 종이로 만들어져 있습니다. 이 무게와 감촉이 바로 원서이지요. 읽기 전에 잠시 그 느낌을 즐겨보세요.

　이미 팔랑팔랑 페이지를 넘겨본 분은 생각보다 분량이 많고 책이 두꺼워서 부담을 느꼈을지도 모르겠네요. 게다가 페이지를 넘기는 중에 모르는 단어가 눈에 들어와 불안해졌을 수도 있습니다. 하지만 걱정할 필요 없어요.

　어떤 문장이든 한 줄 한 줄 제대로 읽지 않으면 그저 뜻 모르는 기호에 불과합니다. 잔뜩 나열된 기호를 보면 누구나 부담을 느낄 수 있어요. 그러므로 걱정하기보다는 차근차근 읽어보세요. 그러다 보면 기호나 다름없던 문자들이 의미 있는 언어로 바뀔 거예요. 어려운지 어떤지는 그때 판단해도 늦지 않습니다.

　사전은 찾아도 되고 안 찾아도 돼요. 뜻풀이를 다는 것도 자유입니다. 스스로 색깔 구분을 하면서 읽어보는 것도 방법이에요. 침대에서 뒹굴면서 읽어도 좋고 과자를 먹으면서 읽어도 상관없습니다. 해서는 안 되는 것, 그런 건 하나도 없어요. 자신에게 맞는 가장 재미있는 방법으로 읽어보세요.

Along came a little girl. She reached inside the box. The weak kitten purred as loud as it could.

Please take me home

그런데 읽어나갈 때 기억해두었으면 하는 것이 있습니다. 영어 대화문에는 아무래도 슬랭(구어체 표현에서 종종 볼 수 있는 비속어)이 나오게 마련이지요. 슬랭은 미국인이라도 전부 이해할 수는 없으니 어느 정도 상상력을 동원해서 읽는 것이 기본이지만, 그래도 불안한 분은 사전을 준비하는 것도 한 방법입니다. 하지만 사전을 이용하는 방법은 되도록 피해주세요. 혹시 사전을 보면서 읽다가 피곤해지거든 주저 없이 사전을 내던지고 나머지는 상상에 맡기세요. 머릿속으로 상황을 그려나가며 구멍을 메워보길 바랍니다. 자주 사용하는 표현이라면 반드시 몇 번씩 나와요. 나올 때마다 의미를 상상하다 보면 어느 순간 의미파악이 가능해집니다. 그러므로 자주 나오지 않는 표현이라면 특별히 암기할 필요는 없습니다. 다시 말해 책을 읽을 때 의미를 알기 힘든 슬랭은 크게 신경 쓰지 말고 읽어나가세요.

또 하나 잊어선 안 될 것이 있습니다. '너무 어렵다'는 판단을 섣불리 내리지 말라는 거예요. '난이도'에도 여러 종류가 있습니다. 단순히 문장이 어려운 경우가 있는가 하면 저자의 개성이나 특징이 묻어나는 문체 자체가 어려운 경우도 있어요. 외국어라면 무조건 어학실력이 부족해서 어렵다고 생각하기 십상이지만, 계속 읽다 보면 난이도가 점점 떨어지는 경우도 많이 있습니다. 왜냐하면 어떤 작가라도 문장의 패턴이나 어휘의 쓰임에 한계를 지니고 있기 때문이에요. 익숙해지면 조금 어려운 문장이라도 술술 읽혀서 뿌듯한 경우도 있으므로, 어렵다고 바로 포기하지 말고 한 페이지라도 더 읽어보려고 노력하길 바랍니다.

서둘러 결론을 내리지 말아야 할 이유는 또 있습니다. 어린이 도서에만 해당되는 이야기가 아니라 어떤 책이든 섣불리 결론을 내리지 말고 끈기있게 책을 읽어나가야 하니까요. 특히 장편소설은 어느 정도 책의 내용에 몰입될 때까지 문장이 잘 머리에 들어오지 않는답니다.

잘 쓰여진 이야기는 이런 부분까지도 배려해서 서두 부분을 집중해서 읽지 못해도 지장이 없도록 구성되어 있습니다. 그러므로 '잘 모르겠다'라고 느껴도 개의치 말고 읽어나가세요. 이는 영어를 읽지 못해서가 아니라 이야기에 몰입이 안 된 탓일 가능성이 크기 때문입니다. 두 번째로 반복해서 읽을 때는 놀랄 만큼 머리에 쏙쏙 들어올 거예요.

책 한 권을 끝까지 읽고 나면 같은 저자가 쓴 다른 작품의 난이도가 훌쩍 떨어져 쉬워질 거예요. 나아가 한 저자의 작품을 대부분 읽고 나면 그 저자가 쓴 장르 자체의 난이도가 떨어져

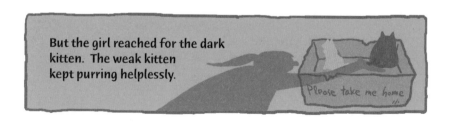

요. 그리고 그 장르의 대표적인 작품을 독파할 때쯤이면 언어 자체의 패턴에 익숙해져서 읽을 수 없는 책이 거의 없어집니다.

기본은 어디까지나 즐기면서 책을 읽는 거예요. 때론 좌절감이 밀려올 수도 있지만 문제 삼을 필요는 없습니다. 그러니 '조금이라도 더 빨리 읽어보자'라든가 '단어를 많이 암기해야지' 라고 생각하지 마세요. 영어책 읽기가 공부가 되어버리는 순간 이야기에 몰입할 수 없게 되므로 단지 지금 눈앞에 펼쳐진 이야기를 즐겨보세요.

모르는 단어나 문장이 많이 나올 거예요. 하지만 신경 쓰지 마세요. 제대로 이해하지 못했더라도 재미를 느낄 수 있도록 쓰어진 책이 어린이 책이니까요.

로알드 달이 쓴 〈Matilda〉라는 작품에 책을 막 읽기 시작한 주인공에게 아래와 같은 구절을 들려주는 장면이 나옵니다.

'잘 모르는 부분은 신경 쓰지 않아도 된단다. 편안한 마음으로 활자가 스스로 걸어다니는 모습을 즐겨보렴, 음악을 들을 때처럼.'

The dark kitten opened one eye and scratched the girl's hand.

Please take me home

STEP 4
~ 책을 다 읽고 나면 ~

자, 드디어 마지막 단계입니다.

처음에 읽은 한 권의 책이 가장 재미있는 책이 된다면 더할 나위 없이 바람직한 일입니다. 하지만 만약 그렇지 못했더라도, 아니 가장 재미있었다고 해도 다시 좋은 책을 계속 찾아보고 싶겠죠. 물론 '기본 세 권'에 이어서 〈Marvin Redpost〉도 읽어보라고 권하고 싶습니다. 특히 앞서 소개한 책을 재미있게 읽은 여러분에게는 반가운 소식이 있습니다.

사실 지금까지 소개한 책은 대부분 시리즈물의 첫 권입니다. 다행히 1권이 재미있었다면 다음 권들도 재미있게 읽을 수 있지요. 그 뒤를 이어 같은 캐릭터, 같은 무대가 등장하기 때문이에요. 시리즈물은 꾸준히 읽어나가면 실제로 친한 친구를 얻은 듯한 느낌이 들어요. 바로 이 점이 시리즈의 장점이라고 할 수 있습니다. 친한 친구와 나누는 이야기라면 영어라도 결코 부담스럽지 않을 거예요.

다음 페이지부터 각 책마다 읽고 난 뒤 선택할 수 있는 도서목록을 실었습니다. 이 도서목록을 참고로 점점 범위를 넓혀가세요. '기본 세 권'을 전부 다 읽고 나면 선택범위도 한결 넓어질 것입니다. 그 다음부터는 마음 가는 대로 책을 골라서 새로운 세계를 즐기길 바랍니다.

So the girl took the weak one instead.

Please take me home

● 로알드 달의 Charlie and the Chocolate Factory를 다 읽은 여러분에게

1. Charlie and the Great Glass Elevator (직접적인 속편)
2. 로알드 달의 장편소설
3. 로알드 달의 단편소설
4. 루이스 새커의 책 (다음 페이지 참조)

〈Charlie and the Chocolate Factory〉를 재미있다고 느낀 분은 행운입니다. 이 이야기의 저자 로알드 달은 세계적으로 유명한 어린이 책 작가 중의 한 사람으로 멋진 작품을 많이 썼습니다. 직접적인 속편으로는 〈Charlie and the Great Glass Elevator〉란 작품이 있고 이외의 다른 작품도 모두 훌륭하지요.

많은 장편 중에서도 특히 권하고 싶은 작품은 소녀 마틸다가 심술궂은 아버지, 그리고 선생님과 한바탕 전쟁을 벌이는 〈Matilda〉와 거인과 여자아이의 모험을 그린 〈THE BFG〉, 거대한 복숭아를 타고 곤충들과 바다 건너 여행을 떠나는 소년을 그린 판타지 〈James and the Giant Peach〉 등이 있습니다.

한편 〈Charlie and the Chocolate Factory〉가 재미는 있어도 너무 길다고 느낀 여러분에게는 단편소설을 권합니다. 단편소설은 장편의 3분의 1 분량으로 부담 없이 읽을 수 있어요. 추천작으로는 부끄럼을 많이 타는 할아버지가 99마리의 거북이를 이용해서 동경하던 여성에게 사랑을 고백하는 기상천외한 이야기 〈Esio Trot〉, 불길하고 우울한 블랙유머의 진수를 보여주는 걸작 〈George's Marvelous Medicine〉, 그리고 지혜로운 아빠 여우가 주인공으로 등장하는, 디즈니 애니메이션을 방불케 하는 작품 〈Fantastic Mr. Fox〉 등의 작품을 들 수 있어요. 장편이든 단편이든 어떤 작품이나 꿈과 희망의 틈새에 슬며시 독을 품고 있으므로 방심하고 있다간 마음이 쿡 찔릴 거예요.

After that, no one came by for a long time.

Please take me home

● 앤드루 클레먼츠의 Frindle을 다 읽은 여러분에게

1. 이외의 클레먼츠 작품
2. 루이스 새커의 책(아래 글 참조)
3. 로알드 달의 책(앞 페이지 참조)

아쉽지만 〈Frindle〉은 직접적인 속편이 없습니다. 하지만 저자 앤드루 클레먼츠는 비슷한 스타일의 작품을 많이 썼어요. 어떤 작품이든 〈Frindle〉의 닉과 닮았지만 약간 변화를 준 소년소녀가 주인공으로 등장하여, 흥미진진한 소재를 중심으로 이야기를 끌어갑니다. 추천작은 컴퓨터와 상상력을 동원해서 최고의 학급신문을 만들려는 〈The Landry News〉, 학교에서 허드렛일을 하는 아버지를 부끄러워하는 소년의 이야기 〈The Janitor's Boy〉, 그리고 같은 반 친구가 쓴 소설을 가지고 마치 어른인 양 에이전트를 가장하여 출판하려고 애쓰는 초등학생 이야기 〈The School Story〉가 있습니다.

클레먼츠의 소설은 초등학교를 무대로 한 작품이 많으므로 좀 더 색다른 분위기를 느끼고 싶다면 루이스 새커나 로알드 달의 책을 읽어보세요. 〈Frindle〉이 마음에 든 분이라면 위에서 말한 어떤 책이라도 취향에 맞을 거예요.

● 루이스 새커의 Someday Angeline을 다 읽은 여러분에게

1. Dogs Don't Tell Jokes(직접적인 속편)
2. 새커의 장편소설
3. 같은 저자의 Wayside School 시리즈
4. 같은 저자의 Marvin Redpost 시리즈

Finally when it was night, the dark kitten woke up and realized it was starving. It stretched and looked around.

Please take me home

〈Someday Angeline〉의 저자 루이스 새커는 현재 미국에서 가장 인기 많은 작가입니다. 그는 권위 있는 아동문학상을 두 개나 동시에 수상한, 사상 최초의 쾌거를 이룬 작가예요. 그 수상작인 〈Holes〉는 독자들의 큰 호응을 얻었습니다. 〈Holes〉는 적극적으로 추천하는 작품이지만 새커의 다른 작품에 비해 상당히 난이도가 높기 때문에 끈기를 가지고 도전해볼 만해요. 이외의 작품도 참신한 스토리와 생생한 캐릭터 그리고 산뜻한 결말로 여러분에게 틀림없이 만족을 줄 거예요.

〈Dogs Don't Tell Jokes〉는 〈Someday Angeline〉에 나온 등장인물의 이후 모습을 그린 후속편입니다. 〈Someday Angeline〉에 등장했던 떠벌이 소년 군이 앤절린의 격려에 힘입어 '사람을 웃기는 것'이 무엇인지 참된 의미를 깨닫는 과정을 그린 이야기예요. 학교축제의 장기자랑에 참가하게 된 군은 웃음을 유발하기 위해 열심히 궁리하는 중에 점차 자신의 내면과 마주하게 돼요. 여러 사람의 아이디어가 반영된 본격적인 장기자랑 현장은 예상을 뒤엎는 전개와 스릴로 손에 땀을 쥐게 합니다. joke가 작품의 주제인 만큼 도중에 이해하기 어려운 장면이 있을 수도 있지만 모르는 대화문은 건너뛰고 읽는다는 각오로 꼭 끝까지 읽어보세요. 최후의 순간 군이 모든 것을 걸고 내놓은 '비밀병기'는 만국 공통의 언어 '웃음'이므로 편안하게 읽으세요. 분량이 많은 책이 부담스럽다면 같은 작가가 쓴 〈Wayside School〉 시리즈를 추천합니다. 2~3쪽 정도 되는 짧은 이야기로 구성된 이 시리즈는 어느 이야기나 마지막에 확실한 결말을 맺기 때문에 지루하지 않아요. 또한 독립된 이야기지만 시리즈 전체가 서로 유기적으로 연관되어 있습니다. 앞에서 소개한 〈Marvin Redpost〉 시리즈도 루이스 새커의 작품으로 〈Someday Angeline〉보다 훨씬 읽기 쉽습니다. 한 권씩 차근차근 읽어나가고 싶은 여러분에게 이 책을 추천합니다.

And then, tore open the box.

1. Marvin Redpost 시리즈를 계속 읽는다
2. 같은 저자의 Wayside School 시리즈
3. 루이스 새커의 다른 작품

〈Marvin Redpost〉는 사실 1권만으로는 참맛을 알 수 없는 시리즈물입니다. 2권부터 점차 흥미진진해지므로 꼭 끝까지 읽어보세요. 권수를 거듭할수록 등장인물이 제대로 갖춰지고 뒤로 갈수록 전체적으로 통일된 전개를 보여주며 무대도 점점 확장됩니다. 끝까지 읽고 나면 틀림없이 평생 동안 잊을 수 없는 시리즈가 될 거예요.

〈Marvin Redpost〉가 벅차다고 느꼈다면 '기본 세 권'으로 돌아가든가 Marvin 시리즈의 저자인 루이스 새커의 다른 작품을 골라보길 바랍니다(앞의 '〈Someday Angeline〉을 다 읽은 여러분에게' 항목 참조).

각 책마다 다 읽고 난 뒤에 읽을 만한 추천도서 목록을 써두었지만 어느 책이든 중요한 또 하나의 선택권이 있습니다. 바로 같은 책을 '다시 읽어보는 것'이에요. 이미 결말을 알고 있는 책을 다시 읽는 것은 지루하다고 생각하기 쉽지만 두 번째이기 때문에 참 재미를 느끼며 책을 읽을 수 있지요. 결말이 어떻게 될지 미리 알고 있으므로 캐릭터에 더욱 치중하여 대사나 행동 묘사 등을 곱씹어볼 수 있으며, 처음에 읽을 때는 미처 눈치 채지 못하던 복선 등 이야기를 전체적으로 파악하지 않으면 보이지 않는 것들을 찾아내는 즐거움을 느낄 수도 있답니다. 마음에 든 책은 반드시 다시 읽어보세요. 좋아하는 장면만 골라 읽어도 상관없습니다.

만약 '기본 세 권' 중에서 고른 책이 어려워서 제대로 앞으로 나아가지 못했다면 나머지 책들을 훑어보세요. '난이도가 비슷하면 결과도 비슷하지 않을까'라고 생각할 수 있지요. 물론 그럴 가능성도 있지만 '책을 읽을 수 있는 힘'이란 난이도뿐 아니라 얼마나 나와 맞느냐도 크

And no one knows
where that kitten is today.

END

Please take me home

게 작용합니다. '기본 세 권'은 각각 미묘한 차이가 있는 이야기이므로 문체에도 상당한 차이가 있어요. 〈Someday Angeline〉을 딱딱하다고 느꼈다면 〈Frindle〉이라면 충분히 읽을 만합니다.

만약 기본 세 권을 전부 별로 읽고 싶지 않다면 〈Marvin Redpost〉를 꼭 읽어보길 바랍니다. 대화 부분은 슬랭이 있어서 다소 까다로울 수도 있지만 이것만 제외하면 아주 읽기 쉬운 작품이에요. 〈Marvin Redpost〉도 전혀 마음에 와 닿지 않았다면 아래 두 권을 읽어보세요. 아래에 소개한 책들은 문장이 아주 읽기 쉬우면서도 동시에 재치가 넘치는 걸작입니다.

Nate the Great by Marjorie Weinman Sharmat

이 작품은 트렌치코트를 걸친 초등학생 네이트 더 그레이트의 차분한 내레이션으로 전개되는 이야기로, 주변에서 일어난 여러 가지 사건을 풀어나가는 미스터리 시리즈입니다. 사건들은 '물건이 없어졌다'거나 '애완동물이 행방불명됐다'는 등 언뜻 보기엔 사소한 사건으로 보이지만 네이트는 언제나 본격적인 수사를 펼쳐서 사건을 깊숙이 파헤쳐요. 내레이션이 추리극 같은 분위기도 물씬 풍깁니다. 오늘도 애견 슬래지와 함께 트렌치코트를 걸치고 팬케이크를 먹으며 수사를 펼치고 있는 네이트의 활약을 직접 찾아보세요.

Amelia Bedelia by Peggy Parish

이 작품은 영어의 관용표현을 익히는 데 안성맞춤입니다. 그도 그럴 것이 이 작품의 주인공인 하녀 아멜리아는 어떤 단어든 표면적인 의미 그대로 받아들이는 여성이에요. 주인의 부탁이라면 뭐든지 충실히 이행하기 때문에 매번 엉뚱한 소동이 일어나고 말아요. 예를 들어 dress the chicken이라고 하면 '닭고기 요리의 밑손질'을 의미하지만, 단어 뜻 그대로 해석하면 '닭고기에 옷을 입히다'란 의미가 돼요. 그러니 아멜리아가 이 말을 들으면…… 어떻게 될지 상상이 될 거예요. 이렇듯 폭소를 자아내는 작품이지만 마지막 장면에서는 훈훈한 온기도 느낄 수 있답니다.

〈Nate the Great〉도 〈Amelia Bedelia〉도 각각 속편이 끊임없이 이어지는 인기 시리즈입니다. 이 두 시리즈는 꼭 1권부터 읽지 않아도 되지만 되도록 처음부터 읽어나갈 것을 권합니다.

〈Nate the Great〉를 다 읽고 나서 좀 더 본격적인 미스터리 작품을 읽고 싶다면 〈Encyclopedia Brown〉이나 〈A to Z Mysteries〉 시리즈를 추천합니다. 전자는 단편을 묶은 미스터리 작품이고 후자는 길이가 중편 정도 되는 읽기 쉬운 시리즈예요. 자세한 소개는 뒤쪽에 수록되어 있습니다.

어떤 방향으로 가든 괜찮습니다. 부디 자유롭게 어린이 도서의 세계를 거닐기 바랍니다.

THE
NEXT STEP
~ 책을 좀 더 찾아본다 ~

책 소개는 거의 마지막 단계입니다. 지금까지 소개한 작품 중에 마음에 든 이야기가 있기를 바라지만 설령 그렇지 못했더라도 포기하지 말고 계속 찾아보길 바랍니다. 여기서 소개한 작품은 수백, 수천, 수만 권의 어린이 책 중에서 불과 몇 권뿐이에요. 그 중에서도 되도록 보편적이고 읽기 쉬운 작품을 선별했어요. 좀 더 무서운 이야기, 초현실적인 이야기, 로맨틱한 이야기 등 어린이 도서는 소재에 제한이 없습니다.

이번에는 이처럼 다양한 어린이 책들을 지면이 허락하는 한 조금이라도 더 소개하고자 합니다.

Goosebumps by R. L. Stine

공포소설 장르에도 명작들이 많이 있습니다. 이 장르를 대표하는 작가로는 R. L. 스타인을 가장 먼저 꼽을 수 있어요. 대히트작인 〈Goosebumps〉('소름'을 의미한다)는 매권 의외의 결말이 펼쳐지는 가벼운 공포소설 시리즈로 현재까지 80권 이상 출간되었어요. 매권마다 완결되는 형식이며 유령의 집부터 UFO까지 다양한 주제를 다루고 있으므로 각 권의 제목을 보고 취향에 맞는 작품을 고르길 바랍니다. 시리즈 중 한 작품만 구입해도 다른 모든 작품의 제목이 실려 있을 거예요. 이 저자는 이외에도 다양한 공포소설 시리즈를 출판하고 있으므로 그 책들도 도전해보세요.

Holes by Louis Sachar

이미 친숙한 루이스 새커의 대표작입니다. 주인공 스탠리 옐넷츠(Stanley Yelnats)는 누명을 뒤집어쓰고 재판을 받은 후 청소년 감호시설 대신 '그린 호수 캠프장'으로 보내져요. 스탠리는 캠프장에서 보내는 생활이 감호시설보다는 나을 것이라고 생각했지만, 막상 '그린 호수 캠프장'에 가보니 호수는 흔적도 찾을 수 없었습니다. 호수의 물은 몇십 년 전에 이미 고갈되었고 불볕더위에 사막으로 변해가는 대지만 끝없이 펼쳐진 황량한 곳. 그곳이 바로 '그린 호수 캠프장'이었지요. 그린 호수 캠프장에 모인 소년들은 인격교정이라는 명목 아래 매일 땅에 구멍을 파야만 했습니다. 그러나 정작 구멍을 파는 이유는 따로 있는 듯……

Ink Drinker by Eric Sanvoisin

이번에는 프랑스 작품으로 암울한 분위기를 풍기는 세련된 판타지 시리즈입니다. 주인공은 책이라면 질색인 소년인데, 어쩔 수 없이 여름방학 동안 아버지가 경영하는 서점에서 일하게 돼요. 서점에서 소년은 주머니에서 빨대를 꺼내 책 속의 활자를 들이마시는 기묘한 남자를 발견합니다. 잠시 후 그 책을 펼쳐보니 백지들만 있습니다. 소년은 호기심에 사로잡혀 남자를 뒤쫓기 시작하는데……

Judy Moody by Megan McDonald

Judy Moody는 자기과시욕이 강한 변덕쟁이 소녀예요. 그녀의 급격한 감정의 변화는 Good Mood, Bad Mood와 같이 간접적이지만 자주 표현됩니다. 디자인이 감각적이고 책 자체가 인테리어 소품이 될 만큼 예쁘답니다. 특히 여성에게 권하고 싶은 작품이에요.

Sammy Keyes by Wendelin Van Draanen

새로운 감각이 돋보이는 탐정 미스터리 시리즈입니다. 중학생인 소녀 사미는 할머니와 단둘이 삽니다. 어머니는 할리우드의 여배우가 되겠다며 집을 나가버렸어요. 고령자 전용 임대 아파트에 무단으로 입주해 있기 때문에 평소 외출도 마음대로 못하는 생활이지만 씩씩한 사미는 굳세게 살아갑니다. 그리고 사미는 기존의 탐정과는 달리 자신이 탐정이라고 생각하지 않아요. 어느 날 무심코 사건에 휘말리고 우연히 수수께끼를 해결하지요. 1권은 아동 미스터리 부문 에드가 상을 수상할 만큼 본격적인 미스터리로 수수께끼를 해결하는 과정도 교묘하고 복잡합니다. 문체가 함축적이므로 지금까지 소개한 책 중에서 가장 난이도가 높지만 미스터리를 좋아하는 분이라면 깜찍하고 매력적인 소녀탐정 사미와 함께하는 모험에 마음을 뺏길 거예요. 시간을 두고 꾸준히 도전해보세요. 처음에는 번역된 책을 읽고 배경과 분위기를 파악한 다음 2권부터 영어로 읽어보는 것도 한 방법입니다.

The Sisterhood of the Traveling Pants by Ann Brashares

마지막으로 소개할 책은 큰 인기를 끈 청춘소설입니다. 단짝친구인 네 명의 소녀가 처음으로 여름방학을 따로 보내게 된 것을 기념하여, 한 벌의 청바지를 돌아가면서 입기로 합니다. 네 사람 중 누가 입어도 신기하게 꼭 맞는 청바지. 어른과 아이의 경계에 선 소녀들이 여름방학 동안 여러 가지 문제에 직면하면서 청바지를 통해 서로 우정을 나누고 훌쩍 성장해가는 모습을 그린 산뜻한 작품이에요. 소녀들이 직면한 문제는 모두 현실적이고 사실적이지만 결코 분위기가 어둡지는 않습니다. 네 명의 소녀가 각각 이야기를 펼쳐가므로 옴니버스 형식에 가깝지요. 난이도는 다소 높지만 다 읽고 나면 가슴 뿌듯한 만족감을 느낄 수 있을 거예요.

Big Fat Cat 시리즈를 쓰기 시작할 때부터 추천도서 목록을 염두에 두고 어린이 책들을 수집하고 계속 읽었습니다. 그러나 꼬리에 꼬리를 물고 재미있는 책이 나오는 바람에 좀처럼 선별하지 못한 채 Big Fat Cat 시리즈가 끝날 무렵이 되어서야 이와 같은 형식으로 소개하게 됐습니다.

서평이나 줄거리에 의존하지 않고 한 권 한 권 직접 음미하면서 정말 재미있다고 생각한 책만을 선별했지만 다소 편향됐을지도 모르겠습니다. 제 바람은 이번에는 여러분 스스로 목록을 만들어보는 것입니다. 어린이 도서에 관한 책이나 인터넷 사이트 등 참고자료는 많이 있습니다. 정보를 수집하고 재미있는 책을 많이 찾아내서 읽어보세요.

어린이 책의 세계는 끝없이 광활한 세계입니다.

영어는 그 세계로 향하는 중요한 열쇠지요.

일단 그 열쇠를 손에 넣으면 언제든 문을 열고 미국의 초등학교로, 초콜릿 공장으로, 용이 사는 마법의 나라로 마음껏 오갈 수 있답니다. 손끝으로 페이지를 넘기기만 하면 늘 새로운 세계로 여행을 떠날 수 있지요.

자, 그 열쇠를 드립니다.

부디 풍요롭고 행복한 여행이 되시길.

THE BIG FAT CAT'S READING LIST

아래의 목록은 기본적으로 가장 저렴한 미국의 페이퍼백을 기준으로 소개했어요. 하지만 색다른 표지나 삽화 등 책의 디자인을 즐기고 싶은 분은 하드커버나 특별판을 구입하길 권합니다. 또 어린이 도서는 대부분 오디오북도 발행하므로 참고하기 바랍니다. 권수가 많은 시리즈는 5권까지만 실었으며 공동저자인 경우 한 사람만 표기했습니다.

1. 짧고 읽기 쉬운 책

Marjorie Weinman Sharmat *Nate the Great*
시리즈는 현재 24권까지 발간되었고, 앞으로도 계속 발간될 예정입니다. 고정 등장인물이 점점 늘어나지만, 결코 순서대로 읽지 않아도 돼요.

Nate the Great Goes Undercover
Nate the Great and the Lost List
Nate the Great and the Phony Clue
Nate the Great and the Sticky Case (이외 다수)

Peggy Parish *Amelia Bedelia*
주인이 손글씨로 남긴 지시사항의 의미에 대해 나옵니다. 관용구나 비유 등 어떤 표현이든 이중적으로 해석이 가능한 문장이에요. 앞으로 나가기 전에 그 문장의 참된 의미와 그 문장을 아멜리아가 어떻게 착각하는지 예상하면서 읽어보면 재미가 두 배로 커질 거예요.

Thank You, Amelia Bedelia
Amelia Bedelia and the Surprise Shower
Come Back, Amelia Bedelia
Play Ball, Amelia Bedelia (이외 다수)

2. 관용표현이 비교적 적은 책

Louis Sachar *Marvin Redpost: Kidnapped at Birth?*
독자들이 앞으로 계속 읽을 것이라 전제하고 쓴 시리즈이므로 2권부터 캐릭터가 제대로 갖춰져서 정말 재미있어집니다. 매권마다 결말은 있으되 전체가 하나의 완성된 이야기이므로 순서대로 읽을 것을 권합니다. 분량도 많지 않아서 술술 읽힐 거예요.

Marvin Redpost: *Why Pick on Me?*
Marvin Redpost: *Is He a Girl?*
Marvin Redpost: *Alone in His Teacher's House*
Marvin Redpost: *Class President*(이외 다수)

Eric Sanvoisin *The Ink Drinker*
문장이 어렵지는 않지만 때때로 변형된 단어가 나옵니다. 하지만 분위기를 연출하기 위해 쓰인 단어이므로 어느 정도 상상력을 동원하거나 건너뛰면서 읽어나가세요.

A Straw for Two
The City of Ink Drinkers
Little Red Ink Drinker(이하 계속 간행)

Donald J. Sobol *Encyclopedia Brown: Boy Detective*
1960년대에 처음 발간된 이래 여전히 소년탐정 소설의 최고봉을 지키고 있는 단편모음 시리즈입니다. 각각의 이야기가 끝날 때마다 독자가 직접 수수께끼를 풀어볼 수 있는 기회가 주어져요.

Encyclopedia Brown and the Case of the Secret Pitch
Encyclopedia Brown Finds the Clues
Encyclopedia Brown Gets His Man
Encyclopedia Brown Solves Them All(이외 다수)

Ron Roy *The Absent Author (A to Z Mysteries)*

아래 목록을 보고 눈치 챈 분도 있겠지만 이 시리즈는 제목이 알파벳 순서대로 배열돼요. 매권 완결되지만 세 소년탐정은 공통으로 등장합니다.

The Bald Bandit (A to Z Mysteries)
The Canary Caper (A to Z Mysteries)
The Deadly Dungeon (A to Z Mysteries)
The Empty Envelope (A to Z Mysteries)(이외 다수)

3. Big Fat Cat 시리즈와 난이도가 거의 비슷한 책

Roald Dahl *Charlie and the Chocolate Factory*

도중에 이탤릭체로 삽입된 시는 상당히 이해하기 어려우므로 건너뛰고 읽어도 돼요. 다른 어린이 책에도 시가 종종 등장하지만 대개 건너뛰고 읽어도 이야기는 충분히 통합니다.

Charlie and the Great Glass Elevator

위 작품의 직접적인 속편입니다. 마찬가지로 찰리가 주인공으로 등장하여 모험을 펼쳐요.

Esio Trot

서문인 Author's Note는 이 작품과 관련해서 작가 자신에 대해 쓴 이야기입니다. 본편과 그다지 관계는 없지만 이 부분만 따로 읽어도 재미있어요.

Fantastic Mr. Fox

삽화가 많고 동물이 주인공으로 나오므로 전래동화와 비슷한 분위기입니다.

George's Marvelous Medicine

로알드 달의 작품 중에서 단연 읽기 쉬운 작품입니다. 삽화가 많고 분위기는 약간 어두워요.

James and the Giant Peach

팀 버튼 감독이 같은 제목으로 영화화했으므로 이미지를 파악하는 데 참고가 될 거예요.(1996년 작품. 영화제목 〈제임스와 거대한 복숭아〉).

The BFG

문장은 간단하지만, 적으로 나오는 거인의 이름 등 만들어진 단어 즉 조어가 많이 나오므로 주의가 필요해요. 낯설고 까다로운 단어가 나오면 일단 두 개의 단어를 합성한 조어가 아닐까 의심해보세요. 참고로 BFG는 문법이 엉터리지만 무슨 말을 하는지는 충분히 이해할 수 있습니다.

Matilda

로알드 달의 작품 중에서 가장 길어요. 서두 부분과 각 장의 첫 부분에 저자의 설명으로 볼 수 있는 글이 포함되어 있습니다. 이 부분만 다소 어려우므로 이해가 잘 안 되면 건너뛰고 읽어보세요.

The Roald Dahl Treasury

단편과 장편을 일부 발췌하여 책으로 엮은 책입니다. 로알드 달의 작품을 몇 번 읽어보고 마음에 들었다면 이 책을 추천해요. 양질의 종이에 다채로운 일러스트가 삽입된 정말 예쁜 책입니다. (단 장편소설은 본편에서 일부만 발췌해서 수록했습니다.)

The Witches

적으로 나오는 Grand High Witch는 말투에 특징이 있습니다. 기본적으로 w를 v로 발음하고 r은 필요 이상으로 강조해서 rrr라고 발음하기도 해요. 혼동하지 마세요.

Louis Sachar *Sideway Stories from Wayside School*

Introduction은 어렵지만 건너뛰고 읽어도 상관없습니다. 전반적으로 독특하고 기발한 내용이므로 '의미를 착각했나?'라는 의심이 들어도 개의치 말고 읽어나가세요. 곧 익숙해질 거예요.

Wayside School is Falling Down
Wayside School Gets a Little Stranger

Sideways Arithmetic from Wayside School
More Sideways Arithmetic from Wayside School

Megan McDonald Judy Moody
주디의 언어라고 할 만큼 변형된 단어가 많이 나오므로 건너뛰고 읽는다는 기분으로 읽어
나가길 바랍니다.

Judy Moody Gets Famous!
Judy Moody Saves the World
Judy Moody Predicts the Future(이하 계속 간행)

Andrew Clements Frindle
사전에서 인용한 부분 등이 이탤릭체로 표기되어 있습니다. 그 부분은 특히 표현이 어렵습
니다. 이해가 되지 않아도 크게 신경 쓰지 마세요.

The Landry News
The School Story
The Janitor's Boy(이외 다수)

R. L. Stine Goosebumps: Welcome to Dead House
이 장편 시리즈는 심령현상, UFO, 괴물, 사이코 서스펜스, 다크 판타지 등 공포소설에 관한
것이라면 뭐든지 적어도 한 번은 다루고 있다고 해도 과언이 아닙니다. 매권마다 결말이 있긴
하지만 시리즈로 이어지는 경우도 있어요.

Goosebumps: Stay Out of the Basement
Goosebumps: Monster Blood
Goosebumps: Say Cheese and Die!
Goosebumps: The Curse of the Mummy's Tomb(이외 다수)

4. 관용표현이 비교적 많은 책

Louis Sachar *Someday Angeline*
  Dogs Don't Tell Jokes
  The Boy Who Lost His Face
  There's a Boy in the Girl's Bathroom

처음의 두 작품(특히 두 번째 작품)에는 joke가 쏟아져 나옵니다. 영어의 특성을 활용한 독특하고 익살스런 표현도 있으므로 한참 생각해봐도 이해가 가지 않을 때는 무시하고 넘어가세요.

남은 두 작품은, 동일한 등장인물이 나오지는 않지만 〈Someday Angeline〉, 〈Dogs Don't Tell Jokes〉와 읽고 난 후의 감상이나 분위기 등이 비슷합니다. 위의 두 권이 마음에 든 분이라면 꼭 읽어보세요.

5. 난이도가 어른용 책 수준으로 높은 책

Louis Sachar *Holes*
  다소 어렵지만 오디오 CD나 영화 DVD 및 번역본 등을 잘 활용하면서 읽어보길 바랍니다.

Wendelin Van Draanen *Sammy Keyes and the Hotel Thief*
  문장 중에 나오는 Grams는 사미의 할머니를 일컫는 애칭입니다. Grandma를 축약한 듯해요. Double Dynamo는 주인공들이 아주 좋아하는 아이스크림의 이름이에요. 등장인물의 이름이 모두 개성있지요. 등장인물을 정리한 표를 만들어서 읽으면 뒷부분의 수수께끼를 풀 때 한결 도움이 될 거예요.
  Sammy Keyes and the Skeleton Man
  Sammy Keyes and the Sisters of Mercy
  Sammy Keyes and the Runaway Elf
  Sammy Keyes and the Curse of Moustache Mary
  (이외 다수, 계속 간행)

Ann Brashares *The Sisterhood of the Traveling Pants*

프롤로그만 조금 어려우므로 벅차다고 느끼면 건너뛰고 읽어도 괜찮습니다. 이야기는 충분히 통해요. 반복해서 다시 읽을 때는 프롤로그도 읽기 쉬울 거예요.

The Second Summer of the Sisterhood

TIPS FROM THE CAT
A DAY IN SCHOOL

어린이 문학작품은 대부분 초등학교나 그 주변이 무대가 됩니다.
고등학교나 대학 풍경은 영화 등에서 종종 나오지만,
초등학교는 좀처럼 나오지 않으니
머릿속에 쉽게 그려지지 않는 장소지요.
그래서 TIPS FROM THE CAT에서는
미국의 초등학교에서 잠시 체험학습을 하려고 합니다.
앞으로 어린이 책을 읽을 때 도움이 될 겁니다.

WELCOME TO GRADE SCHOOL

PLAYGROUND
운동장은 대부분 잔디가 깔려 있습니다. 일주일에 몇 번은 운동장 한복판의 국기게양대 앞에 전교생이 모여 가슴에 손을 얹고 *Pledge of Allegiance to the Flag*(국기에 대한 경례)를 복창합니다.
쉬는 시간이나 체육시간에는 주로 농구나 배구 등 구기운동을 주로 하고 아이들의 경쟁심과 팀워크를 기르는 데 중점을 둡니다.

FENCE
담장 주변에 안전을 위한 튼튼한 울타리를 둘러쳐서 외부와 차단합니다.

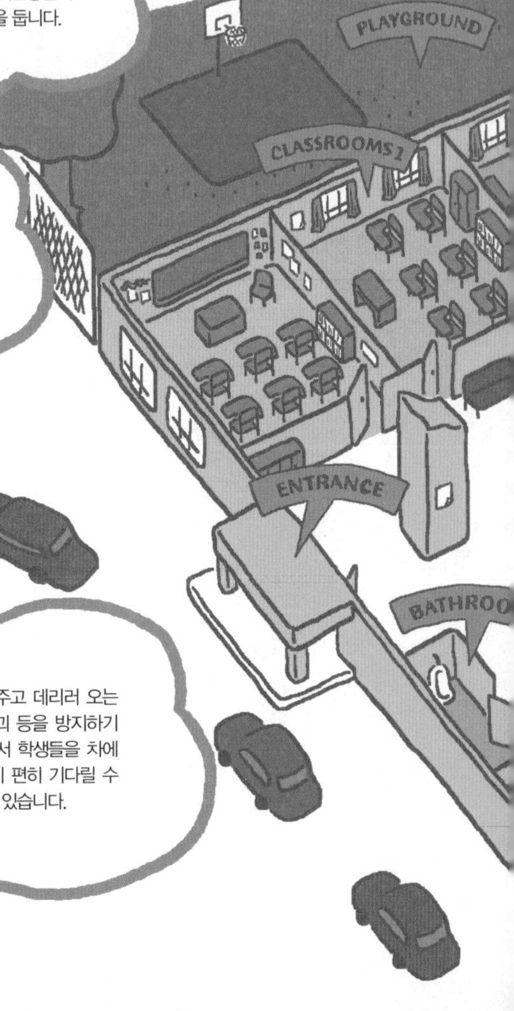

CLASSROOMS 1
1층의 현관 근처에는 저학년 교실이 있습니다. 저학년은 비교적 규율도 엄격하고 대개 책상도 줄을 꼭 맞추어 배치합니다. 고학년으로 올라갈수록 학생들의 자율에 맡겨요.

BULLETIN BOARD
눈에 잘 띄는 장소에 게시판을 두어 매일 등교할 때마다 볼 수 있도록 합니다.

ENTRANCE
등하교시에는 도로 한편에 아이들을 데려다주고 데리러 오는 학부모의 차가 일렬로 늘어서 있습니다. 유괴 등을 방지하기 위해서 선생님이 학부모의 얼굴을 확인하면서 학생들을 차에 태워요. 부모님이 데리러 올 때까지 아이들이 편히 기다릴 수 있도록 교문 근처에는 으레 벤치가 많이 놓여 있습니다.

PLAYGROUND

CLASSROOMS 1

ENTRANCE

BATHROO

우리나라는 초등학교의 교육방침에 대한 주도권이 국가에 있지만, 미국은 주나 시 단위 등 지방자치체제로 관리하고 있습니다. 따라서 지역에 따라 빈부의 차가 심하고 시설과 환경도 학교에 따라 현저히 차이가 납니다. 가장 가난한 지역은 종이나 펜 같은 문방구조차 정기적으로 담임선생님이 학생들에게 사서 주기도 해요. 이것이 현실입니다. (이를 위한 특별감세제도가 있을 정도입니다.) 여기 소개하는 초등학교는 중급 정도에 속하는 초등학교로 평균적인 환경이지만 어디까지나 한 예에 불과합니다. 이 그림에는 어느 초등학교에서나 볼 수 있는 최소한의 시설만 그렸습니다. 대부분의 학교는 여기에 나온 시설 외에 **Gymnasium**(체육관), **Science Room**(과학실), **Music Room**(음악실) 등을 갖추고 있습니다.

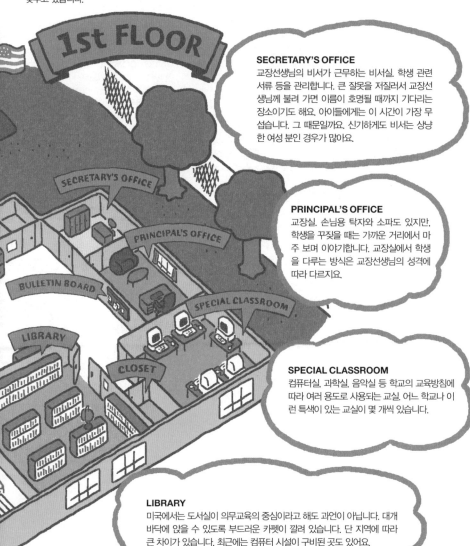

SECRETARY'S OFFICE
교장선생님의 비서가 근무하는 비서실. 학생 관련 서류 등을 관리합니다. 큰 잘못을 저질러서 교장선생님께 불려 가면 이름이 호명될 때까지 기다리는 장소이기도 해요. 아이들에게는 이 시간이 가장 무섭습니다. 그 때문일까요. 신기하게도 비서는 상냥한 여성 분인 경우가 많아요.

PRINCIPAL'S OFFICE
교장실. 손님용 탁자와 소파도 있지만, 학생을 꾸짖을 때는 가까운 거리에서 마주 보며 이야기합니다. 교장실에서 학생을 다루는 방식은 교장선생님의 성격에 따라 다르지요.

SPECIAL CLASSROOM
컴퓨터실, 과학실, 음악실 등 학교의 교육방침에 따라 여러 용도로 사용되는 교실. 어느 학교나 이런 특색이 있는 교실이 몇 개씩 있습니다.

LIBRARY
미국에서는 도서실이 의무교육의 중심이라고 해도 과언이 아닙니다. 대개 바닥에 앉을 수 있도록 부드러운 카펫이 깔려 있습니다. 단 지역에 따라 큰 차이가 있습니다. 최근에는 컴퓨터 시설이 구비된 곳도 있어요.

미국의 초등학교에선 대부분 명확한 시간의 구분이 없습니다. 각 반의 담임선생님 재량에 따라 개별적으로 시간표를 짜요. 예를 들어 책상의 배치도 엄한 선생님은 우리나라의 초등학교처럼 줄을 맞춰서 정렬하지만, 아이들의 자율성을 존중하는 선생님은 파격적인 배치를 하기도 합니다. 이 학교도 고학년 교실은 배치가 특이합니다. 4학년은 책상을 없애고 선생님을 중심으로 바닥에 둘러앉아 수업을 진행하고, 5학년은 책상을 원형으로 배치했어요. 6학년이 되면 책상마다 칸막이를 부착해서 학생들이 방을 꾸미듯이 나름대로 장식을 합니다. 또 책상배치에 따라 생긴 통로도 *Main Street*과 같이 학생들이 자유롭게 이름을 붙이고요.

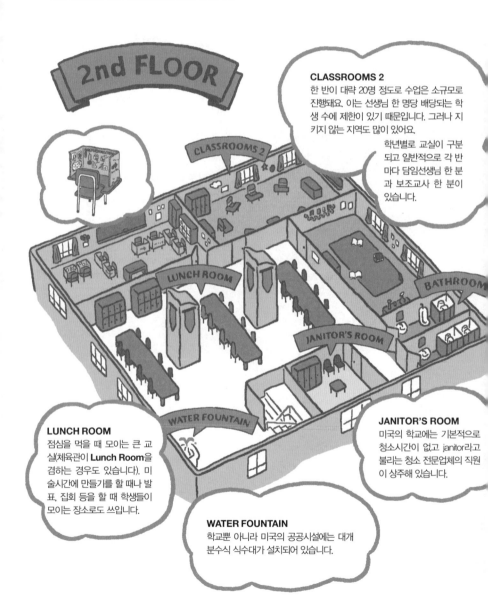

2nd FLOOR

CLASSROOMS 2

LUNCH ROOM

BATHROOM

JANITOR'S ROOM

WATER FOUNTAIN

CLASSROOMS 2
한 반이 대략 20명 정도로 수업은 소규모로 진행돼요. 이는 선생님 한 명당 배당되는 학생 수에 제한이 있기 때문입니다. 그러나 지키지 않는 지역도 많이 있어요.

학년별로 교실이 구분되고 일반적으로 각 반마다 담임선생님 한 분과 보조교사 한 분이 있습니다.

LUNCH ROOM
점심을 먹을 때 모이는 큰 교실(체육관이 Lunch Room을 겸하는 경우도 있습니다). 미술시간에 만들기를 할 때나 발표, 집회 등을 할 때 학생들이 모이는 장소로도 쓰입니다.

JANITOR'S ROOM
미국의 학교에는 기본적으로 청소시간이 없고 janitor라고 불리는 청소 전문업체의 직원이 상주해 있습니다.

WATER FOUNTAIN
학교뿐 아니라 미국의 공공시설에는 대개 분수식 식수대가 설치되어 있습니다.

선생님과 학부모 간의 연락은 대부분 손으로 쓴 메모를 통해 이루어 집니다. 조퇴하거나 부모님이 데리러 오는 시간이 늦어질 때는 부모님이 써주신 메모를 선생님께 전달하고, 학생이 잘못을 저지르면 선생님은 그 내용을 메모해서 학생에게 부모님 사인을 받아오라고 합니다. 부모님이 확인을 한 후에는 다음날 학교에 다시 가지고 와야 해요.

예외도 있지만 대부분의 초등학교에서 교과서는 학교에서 빌려주는 방식입니다. 미국의 교과서는 대개 분량이 두꺼워서 매일 들고 다니기에는 부담스럽습니다. 따라서 학교 사물함이나 책상서랍에 교과서를 두고 다녀요. 그래서 교과서는 낙서투성이거나 파손되어 있는 등 그다지 상태가 좋지 않아요.

선생님이 학생을 부를 때는 대개 **Ed**라고 이름을 부르지만, 꾸중을 할 때는 성에다 존칭을 붙여서 **Mr. Wishbone**이라고 부릅니다. 후자로 불릴 때면 아이들은 바짝 긴장하게 마련이지요.

대부분의 초등학교에서는 점심시간에 집에서 준비해온 도시락을 먹거나 미리 학교에 **hot lunch**를 주문해둡니다. *hot lunch*는 매달 초에 식단표를 배부해요. 주요 메뉴는 치킨 너겟, 스파게티, 볶음밥, 터키 샌드위치 등입니다. 여기에 채소 한 접시와 파이나 케이크 등 후식이 첨부돼요. 가격은 매우 저렴하지만, 그만큼 맛은 별로 기대할 수 없지요.

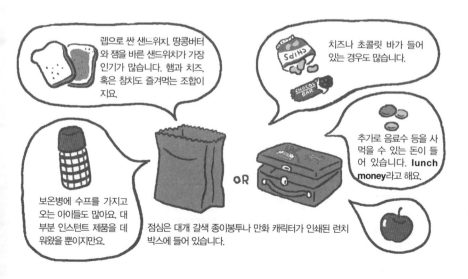

랩으로 싼 샌드위치. 땅콩버터와 잼을 바른 샌드위치가 가장 인기가 많습니다. 햄과 치즈, 혹은 참치도 즐겨먹는 조합이지요.

치즈나 초콜릿 바가 들어 있는 경우도 많습니다.

추가로 음료수 등을 사 먹을 수 있는 돈이 들어 있습니다. **lunch money**라고 해요.

보온병에 수프를 가지고 오는 아이들도 많아요. 대부분 인스턴트 제품을 데워왔을 뿐이지만요.

점심은 대개 갈색 종이봉투나 만화 캐릭터가 인쇄된 런치박스에 들어 있습니다.

BIG FAT CAT'S
3 COLOR
DICTIONARY

BIG FAT CAT
and the
FORTUNE COOKIE

빅팻캣의 3색사전

~빅팻캣과 포춘 쿠키 편~

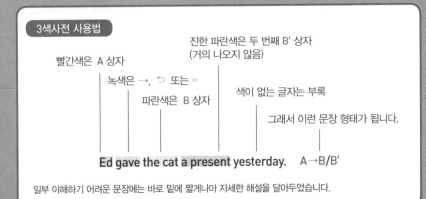

3색사전 사용법

빨간색은 A 상자

진한 파란색은 두 번째 B′ 상자
(거의 나오지 않음)

녹색은 →, ↰ 또는 =

색이 없는 글자는 부록

파란색은 B 상자

그래서 이런 문장 형태가 됩니다.

Ed gave the cat a present yesterday.   A→B/B′

일부 이해하기 어려운 문장에는 바로 밑에 짧게나마 자세한 해설을 달아두었습니다.

3색사전은 스토리 부분의 영문을 색깔로 구분하여 문형을 한눈에 알아볼 수 있도록 만든 힌트북입니다.
물론 '정답'은 아닙니다. 영문을 이해하기 위한 하나의 길잡이로 이용해주시기 바랍니다.

p.5

"Yes." 불완전한 문장

"**The contracts are signed.** A=B
본문 5~6쪽에 나오는 대화문은 모두 제레미 아버지가 전화기에 대고 하는 말입니다. 상대의 목소리는 들리지 않아요.

I want that street **torn down** by the end of next month. A→B=B'
that street=torn down한 상태가 되기를 제레미 아버지가 원하고 있습니다.

Yes, the one they call 'Ghost Avenue.'" 불완전한 문장
one은 street의 대역이에요.

" **You did** well with that shopping mall in Old Everville... A↩

Yes, that Out-something Mall. **Wait.**" 불완전한 문장 (A)↩
에드에게 소중한 일터였던 Outside Mall은 제레미 아버지에게는 'Out 어쩌고 ~' 정도로밖에 기억나지 않는, 수많은 개발지 중의 하나일 뿐입니다.

p.6

Jeremy Lightfoot Senior pressed a button on the phone and switched lines.
A→B and (A)→B   line이란 전화선을 일컫습니다. 'line을 switch했다'는 뜻은 이전 통화는 잠깐 보류로 두고 다른 상대와 연결했다는 것이에요.

"Yes? I see ... 불완전한 문장 A↩

All right. Good. 불완전한 문장 불완전한 문장

Oh, and one more thing. 불완전한 문장

If my son happens to win the contest, tell the judges he was responsible for Wishbone's problems." (A)→B/B'
If에서 쉼표까지는 '만일 ~한다면'이란 의미지만 건너뛰고 읽어도 상관없습니다. happens to win은 '이기는 상황이 일어난다'예요.

"Yes, Disqualify him" 불완전한 문장 (A)→B

p.7

"Okay. How many pies now?" 불완전한 문장   불완전한 문장

The host stuck his head behind the curtain of the judges' booth and asked a
staff member.   A→B and (A)→B

The staff member was busy running around with pies in his hands.   A=B

He shouted to the host.   A↺

"Sixteen. Almost done!"   불완전한 문장   불완전한 문장

"Okay. Time?"   불완전한 문장   불완전한 문장

"Thirty seconds and counting."   불완전한 문장
> 카운트다운이 진행되는 짧은 순간에도 마감시간이 점점 임박해오고 있습니다. 따라서
> ~ and counting을 붙여서 '현재 시각은 ~지만 지금도 시간이 흘러가고 있다'라는 의미
> 를 표현했어요.

"Got it," the host said as he stepped back onto the stage.   A→B

"LADIES AND GENTLEMEN!   불완전한 문장

Thirty more seconds!   불완전한 문장

Most of the pies are finished, and the battle is coming to an end!
A=B and A=B

This is Robert R. Silverman.   A=B

Welcome back to the PIEGAMES!"   불완전한 문장

p.8

"Thirty seconds!?"   불완전한 문장

George looked back at Ed.   A→B

"Did he say thirty seconds?!"   A→B

"Don't stop! Keep going!" Ed shouted back to George, as he shook a
saucepan full of blueberries.   A→B
> Keep going은 'go하는 동작을 유지하라' 다시 말해 '계속해!'란 의미지만, 오히려 '멈추
> 지 마!'란 뉘앙스가 강합니다.

They were the only ones still baking.   A=B

Most of the other contestants were cleaning up their booths.   A=B

A lot of people in the audience were laughing and pointing at them.   A=B

"Twenty seconds!" the host announced.   A→B

Ed was covered with food — whipped cream on his head, flour spread over
    his shirt, and blueberry stains on his sleeves.   A=B

"*Ten!*"   불완전한 문장

The host cried, and the audience joined in.   A↻, and A↻

"*Nine!*" they called out together.   A→B

p.9

Ed's hands were shaking badly.   A=B

He tried to calm down but couldn't.   A→B but (A)↻

The whole world seemed to spin around him.   A=B

"Ed! There's no time!" George cried out in panic.   A→B

Ed dashed to the table with his saucepan.   A↻

But he moved too fast.   A↻

He slipped and the saucepan flew through the air.   A↻ and A↻

"*Five!*" the crowd counted.   A→B

Ed and George both tried to catch the saucepan.   A→B

They both failed.   A↻

The blueberries in the saucepan scattered all over the floor.   A↻

Some of them splashed on Ed.   A↻

"*Three!*"   불완전한 문장

Ed and George stared at each other.   A→B

"Two!" 불완전한 문장

Ed closed his eyes.　A→B

"One!" 불완전한 문장

p.10

"BeeJees?" 　불완전한 문장

Frank peeked at BeeJees to check if he was asleep. 　A→B

이 문장에서 he는 비지스의 대역입니다. 비지스가 asleep하고 있는지 어떤지 프랭크가 들여다보고 있어요.

He was. 　A=(B)

He was asleep의 줄임형입니다.

Frank shrugged, and drove his wagon past BeeJees, whistling a tune from a cartoon show.　A⤴, and (A)→B

"Yaba daba daba... Yaba daba dooo..." 　불완전한 문장 　불완전한 문장

Willy had finally stopped shaking a while ago, and BeeJees had fallen asleep from exhaustion.　A→B, and A⤴

Frank had come over to see if he was all right.　A⤴

come은 단순히 땅 위를 밟아 이동하는 이미지인 데 비해, over가 붙으면 커다란 손이 Frank를 훌쩍 들어올려 A 지점에서 B 지점으로 이동시킨 이미지가 돼요. run over, walk over, move over 등 동작에 over가 붙는 형태는 전부 해당돼요. he는 여기서도 비지스의 대역이에요. 밤새 간병을 한 비지스가 all right한지 프랭크는 확인하고 싶었던 거예요.

p.11

Something cracked beneath Frank's wagon.　A⤴

Frank bent down and found one of Willy's fortune cookies stuck under the front wheel.　A⤴ and (A)→B=B'

He reached down and picked it up.　A⤴ and (A)→B

The fortune paper was sticking out.　　A=B

He pulled it out and took a look.　　A→B and (A)→B

"Mi... Mira..."　　불완전한 문장

Frank tried to read it, but gave up.　　A→B, but (A)↺

He laid the paper down gently beside Willy, and went back to the fire.
　　A→B, and (A)↺

Some friends of Willy's had gathered a pile of wood for them.　　A→B

Frank started adding wood to the fire.　　A→B

Unnoticed by anyone, Willy's hand moved slightly.　　A↺

It touched the fortune paper Frank had set beside him.　　A→B
　　Frank 이하의 문장은 fortune paper의 화장문입니다.

The paper reflected the flickering red light of the campfire.　　A→B

Once, twice, it glowed.　　A↺

Then a gust of wind blew it into the fire, and it disappeared forever.
　　A→B, and A↺

"Aaaand it's over!!"　　A=B p.12

The host raised his hand and announced aloud.　　A→B and (A)↺

Most of the contestants threw their hats and aprons up into the air and
　　hugged each other.　　A→B and (A)→B

The audience applauded hard and the pie contest came to an end.
　　A↺ and A↺

Ed was still holding the eggbeater in his hand.　　A=B
　　eggbeater는 본문 8쪽의 삽화에서 에드가 오른손에 들고 있는 달걀 거품기를 가리켜요.

He had squeezed his eyes shut and was frozen in that position.
　　A→B and (A)=B

George wanted to say something to Ed, but couldn't.　A→B, but (A)↺

All he could do was stare at the clock tower.　A=B

> he는 조지의 대역으로 All he could do는 '그가 할 수 있는 모든 일'이란 의미입니다. 조
> 지가 할 수 있는 일이라고는 B 상자의 행위뿐이었어요.

Two half-finished pies lay on the table.　A↺

Ed and George sat silently on the floor as everyone else ran around them.
A↺　　everyone else란 에드와 조지를 제외한 전원으로 주로 콘테스트에 참가한 경쟁
> 자를 가리킵니다.

"Shucks," George licked the blueberry on his finger and mumbled to
　himself.　A→B and (A)→B

"And it tastes so good too."　A↺

"Wishbone."　　불완전한 문장

Ed looked up.　A↺

It was Jeremy Lightfoot Jr.　A=B

He had taken off his costume.　A→B

He stood there staring at the unfinished pies.　A↺

All around them, the contest staff was busy getting ready for the presentation
　of the pies.　A=B

p.13

Jeremy broke off a piece of Ed's unfinished pie, tasted it, and stared vacantly
　at the rest of the pie.　A→B, (A)→B, and (A)→B

"Wishbone...　　불완전한 문장

About that *trouble* you had..."　　불완전한 문장

Ed shook his head and got up.　A→B and (A)↺

Purple syrup dripped from his shirt.　A↺

"It doesn't matter anymore," Ed said.　A→B

It은 제레미가 앞에서 말한 내용을 가리킵니다. matter는 '관심이 있다'란 뜻으로 이 문장에서는 does not을 붙여 부정하고 있으므로 '(이제) 어떻게 되든 상관없다'란 뉘앙스를 지녀요.

"The contest's over."   A=B

He wiped blueberries off his forehead and started to walk past Jeremy.
    A→B and (A)→B

But Jeremy caught him by the arm.   A→B
    제레미는 에드를 caught(붙들다)하려고 에드의 팔을 잡았습니다.

"Listen, Wishbone.   (A)↺

    I need to tell you something."   A→B

Jeremy jerked Ed back.   A→B

But before he could start talking, Jeremy saw the despair in Ed's eyes and closed his mouth.   A→B and (A)→B

"Ladies and gentlemen..."   불완전한 문장

A voice from the speakers echoed above Ed's head.   A↺

It was the owner of the New Mall.   A=B

"I think it's time to decide our winner."   A→B

Ed silently took Jeremy's hand from his arm.   A→B

He forced himself to smile.   A→B=B'

"It's too late.   A=B

This was the one time I couldn't fail... no matter what — but I did."
    A=B but A↺   no matter what은 '무슨 일이 일어나든 상관없이'라는 강경한 표현입니다. '(이번에는) 실패하면 안 되는 one time이었다'고 말한 뒤 but I did (fail)이라며 에드가 자신을 꾸짖고 있어요.

Ed couldn't keep smiling any more, so he closed his eyes.   A→B, so A→B

"It's over. Nothing can save us now."   A=B   A→B

p.14

Wrong. 불완전한 문장

왜 Wrong(틀리다)이라고 했는지 추측해보세요. 앞에 나오는 마지막 대화문 Nothing can save us now가 Wrong이라고 말하고 있어요. 단어를 생략해서 영어의 절제미를 살린 표현입니다.

p.16

"Holy Jesus Christ in heaven!!" 불완전한 문장

The owner almost had a heart attack as he took a look backstage.　A→B

He staggered and almost fell, but somehow kept standing.
　　A↻ and (A)↻, but (A)→B

He continued to stare at the incredible mess behind the curtains.　A→B

It looked like a miniature hurricane had run through the pies.　A=B

After recovering from the first wave of shock, the owner realized he was still
　　holding the microphone in his hand.　A→B

He gulped, then spoke into it slowly.　A↻, then (A)↻
　　이 문장의 it은 microphone의 대역입니다.

"Um... Ladies and gentlemen, I'm... I'm really sorry.　A=B

I think there's been... an *accident* backstage."　A→B

The owner could hear the audience stir as he said these words.　A→B=B'

He looked around the booth again.　A↻

Almost all of the pies had been completely destroyed.　A=B

He had no choice but to continue.　A→B
　　no choice but ~은 '~하는 이외에 달리 선택권이 없다'는 뜻이에요. 오너는 어쩔 수 없이 이 말을 이어가야만 했지요.

"Um... I'm sorry.　A=B

We may have to cancel the contest."　A→B
　　have to는 'to 이하의 일을 예정 중에 가지고 있다' 다시 말해 '해야만 한다'는 의미로, 이제는 익숙한 표현이겠죠. 이 문장에서는 '어쩌면'이란 의미가 있는 may를 붙여 표현을 다소 순화했어요. 파이가 이 상태로는 콘테스트를 진행할 수 없는 것이 당연하죠.

The main tent had become a confused riot.　A=B　p.17

**The owner and a few other staff members were trying to explain to the angry
audience what had happened, but they were not succeeding.**
A=B, but A=B　　they는 오너와 스태프들의 대역입니다. 관객들을 납득시킬 만한 설명을 하는 데 succeed(성공하다)하지 못했다는 의미예요. 다음 문장에도 나와 있듯이 그들 자신도 무슨 일이 일어났는지 전혀 알 수 없었기 때문이지요.

**This was no surprise, because they had no idea themselves what had
happened.**　A=B, because A→B

**One staff member claimed he had seen "something like an incredibly fast
bowling ball run out of the booth," but that was all they knew.**
A→B, but A=B　　that은 " " 안의 부분을 가리키는 대역이고, they는 오너와 스태프들을 가리켜요.

**The owner and the staff offered a rematch sometime next year, but that just
made everyone angrier.**　A→B, but A→B=B'
that은 that 바로 앞부분의 내용을 가리키는 대역입니다.

**Ed, George, and Jeremy stood watching in silence as everyone fussed and
shouted about the sudden developments.**　A↺

Ed took off his bandanna and stuck it in his pocket.　A→B and (A)→B

He started to walk away.　A→B

"Where are you going, Wishbone?" Jeremy asked.　A→B

Ed didn't respond.　A↺　p.18

He just walked out the back door.　A↺

George and Jeremy stared at each other after the door closed.   A→B

In a corner near the judges' booth, the owner stood surrounded by angry contestants demanding a better answer.   A↺

> surrounded 이하는 오너가 처한 상황을 설명하는 화장문입니다. 콘테스트 참가자들이 a better answer를 요구하고 있어요.

Everything was in chaos.   A=B

The contest is falling apart, Jeremy thought.   A→B

Just as Father would have wanted.   불완전한 문장

> 이탤릭체로 쓰여진 문장은 Jeremy thought가 중간에 삽입되어 있지만 실제로는 하나의 문장입니다. Father가 want한 내용이 앞부분에 해당해요. 아버지의 뜻대로 되어버린 결과에 제레미가 분개하고 있는 듯해요.

In his mind, he heard his father laughing.   A→B=B'

Everything always seemed to end as his father had planned.   A=B

He was sick and tired of it.   A=B

> it은 앞 문장 전체를 가리키는 대역입니다. sick and tired는 '질려버렸다'는 뉘앙스로 몹시 싫어진 경우에 잘 쓰이는 표현이에요.

Jeremy walked over to the judges' booth, picked up a microphone, and switched it on.   A↺, (A)→B, and (A)→B

p.19

"So why don't we do it now?"   A→B

> it은 rematch의 대역입니다. 왜 지금 rematch를 하지 않는지 제레미가 모두에게 묻고 있어요.

Jeremy's voice boomed out of the speakers.   A↺

Almost everyone stopped moving and talking.   A→B

They all looked at Jeremy.   A→B

Jeremy spoke through the microphone again.   A↺

"The rematch. Why don't we do it now?"   불완전한 문장   A→B

A long pause followed, and then one of the contestants shouted.
　　A⤸, and A⤸

"Yeah, why not now?"　불완전한 문장
　　참가자 중의 한 명이 Why로 시작하는 짧은 제레미의 대화문을 반복하고 있습니다.

That was the cue.　A=B

Everyone started agreeing all at once.　A→B

The contestants began shouting for a rematch and the cries from the stands
　　became even more fierce.　A→B and A=B

George looked across the arena at Jeremy.　A→B

Jeremy shrugged and laid down the microphone.　A⤸ and (A)→B

The owner was overwhelmed by the reaction of the crowd.　A=B

He exchanged glances with the judges.　A→B

"Uh... Let us consider this for a moment, please."　(A)→B=B'

The audience kept chanting "Rematch! Rematch!" over and over, louder and
　　louder, until there was no other sound in the stadium.　A→B
　　Rematch라는 음성 외에는 other sound가 들리지 않을 정도로 관객들이 한목소리로
　　외쳤습니다.

"A rematch?"　불완전한 문장

p.20

Ed said to George with a bewildered look.　A⤸

He had been standing alone outside the main tent.　A=B

George had come running over to him with the news.　A⤸

Ed asked again, "A rematch? Why?"　A→B

"The pies were all destroyed. They don't know why," George explained.
　　A→B　why를 이해하기 어려우면 the reason(이유)으로 바꿔보세요.

"But everyone agreed on a second round.　A⤸

We're back in business, Ed!"   A=B

back in business는 문자 그대로 번역하면 '판매재개'지만, business 이외의 상황에서 도 '한번 더 해보자'는 격려의 외침으로 많이 쓰이는 표현입니다.

Ed had a look of pure surprise for a moment, but then he gradually lowered his eyes and nodded.   A→B, but A→B and (A)↺

George was almost dancing around, but he stopped when he noticed that Ed wasn't happy.   A=B, but A↺

"What's the matter?   A=B

matter는 '관심이 있다'는 뜻이고 여기서는 '무엇에 관심이 있지?' 즉 '신경 쓰이게 하는 일이 있어?'라는 의미가 돼요.

We just got another chance, didn't we?"   A→B

"Yup," Ed said in a tired voice.   A→B

"I know."   A↺

But he said nothing more.   A=B

George looked worried.   A=B

"Are you okay?   A=B

Want me to get you a cup of coffee or something?"   (A)→B=B'

조지답게 생략해서 말하고 있습니다. 본래는 Do you want me to ~란 형태로 의문문이에요.

"Thanks. But no thanks," Ed said.   A→B

p.21

"What's wrong, man?   A=B

Isn't this great news?"   A=B

Ed sighed and looked at George with a sad smile.   A↺ and (A)→B

"George. You saw that pie we made.   불완전한 문장   A→B

I was stupid to think we really had a chance to win."   A=B

에드가 think한 내용은 we 이하 부분입니다. chance to win은 '이길 기회'란 뜻이에요.

George's usually happy face clouded over. A⤵

Ed saw this and felt a tinge of guilt. A→B and (A)→B

He looked away. A⤵

"Even if I'd made the pie right, it was just a regular fruit pie. A=B
Even은 '비록'이란 의미로 강조하기 위해 쓰였지만, 이해하기 어려우면 건너뛰고 읽어도 돼요. I'd는 I had의 줄임형입니다.

Nothing special. 불완전한 문장

I'm sorry, George. A=B

You saw all those other pies. A→B

You know we don't have any chance of winning." A→B

"But you *will* win," George said abruptly. A→B

"I know you'll win." A→B

"George..." Ed said, hearing the sincerity in George's voice. A→B

George's trust in him was so genuine it scared him. A=B (that) A→B
마지막 부분에 나오는 it scared him은 별도의 문장으로 파악해도 상관없습니다. it은 앞 부분(조지가 에드를 진심으로 신뢰하고 있다는 사실)을 가리키는 대역이에요.

"Thanks, but sorry. I... I'm really sorry." 불완전한 문장 A=B

Overhead, an announcement echoed from the speakers. A⤵

"...the PIEGAMES will restart at three o'clock, after a one hour break. A⤵

During the break, contestants will be allowed to get extra supplies. A=B

We are very sorry for the inconvenience. A=B

If you choose not to watch the rematch, full refunds for your tickets will be..." A=(B)

p.22

Ed looked away towards the Ferris wheel.　A↺

Ferris wheel에서 첫 글자가 대문자인 이유는 발명가 George W. Ferris의 이름에서 따온 명칭이기 때문입니다.

George realized he was about to walk away, and **tried** desperately **to say something to stop** him — anything that would cheer him up, anything that would tell him how much George appreciated him.

A→B, and (A)→B　　he는 에드의 대역입니다. anything that이란 문구를 두 번 써서 각각 '에드를 격려할 수 있는 무언가', '얼마나 에드에게 고마워하는지 전할 수 있는 무언가'를 조지가 말해보려고 필사적으로 궁리하는 모습을 나타냈어요.

But **this was** too difficult for George.　A=B

여기서의 this는 앞에 나오는 긴 문장을 받아 '에드를 stop시킬 만한 말을 하는 것'을 가리키는 대역이에요.

The truth was, he really believed that Ed would win.　A=B

He just **didn't know why.**　A→B

이 문장의 why도 the reason으로 바꾸면 이해하기 쉽습니다.

"Ed!" **George cried** out helplessly.　A→B

"Your pies are the best!" **he said.**　A→B

"The best in the world! I _know_ it!"　불완전한 문장　A→B

George kept shouting even after Ed had disappeared into the crowd.　A→B

"**Your pies are the best!**　A=B

I know it! I know it!"　A→B　A→B

p.23 **The Ferris wheel was** slowly rotating through the winter sky as Ed walked beneath it.　A=B

He came to the far end of the carnival grounds and **leaned** on the outer fence.
A↺ and (A)↺

Hands in his pockets, **he watched the Ferris wheel go** around.　A→B=B'

His thoughts went around with it, around and around, almost as if he were hypnotized.　Aↄ

There are chances, and there are consequences.　A=B, and A=B

The fortune cookie had said.　Aↄ

He wondered whether the rematch was the chance or the consequence.
　　A→B　　whether는 두 가지 중에서 어느 쪽일지를 가리키는 단어입니다. 이 문장에서는 rematch가 chance일지 consequence일지 에드가 자신에게 묻고 있어요.

He wondered if it even mattered.　A→B
　　it은 앞 문장에 나오는 whether 이하로 에드의 생각을 가리키는 대역입니다. rematch가 chance든 consequence든 '어느 쪽이든 상관없다'고 생각할 정도로 에드는 침체되어 있어요.

You have no idea what a pie is made of.　A→B

Willy had said, but now **he heard it** in his own voice.　Aↄ, but A→B
　　it은 앞 문장에 나오는 '윌리가 전에 했던 말'을 가리키는 대역이에요.

An endless stream of people walked past him.　Aↄ

Some were families, some were couples, and **some were alone.**
　　A=B, A=B, and A=B

It was fascinating just to imagine all of the different lives, different problems, different feelings, and different tastes these people had.　A=B
　　이 문장의 It은 just to imagine 이하입니다. 즉 '에드가 스쳐 지나가는 사람들을 보며 떠올린 상념'을 가리켜요.

It seemed crazy to make a pie that everyone would like.　A=B　p.24
　　It은 to 이하의 대역입니다. 이 문장도 앞의 문장처럼 실제 주인공이 너무 길어서 대신 It을 A 상자에 넣었어요. that 이하는 pie를 꾸며주는 화장문으로, '모든 사람이 좋아하는 파이'란 뜻이에요.

It was like finding a puzzle piece that fit every spot in the puzzle.　A=B

It seemed impossible.   A=B

Ed spotted a balloon floating above the Ferris wheel.   A→B

His mind wandered away with it.   A↺

Bake your pie.   (A)→B

Willy had said.   A↺

He thought he was doing that, but now he wasn't so sure.   A→B, but A=B

그 that은 두 문장 앞에서 '윌리가 에드에게 한 충고'를 가리키는 대역입니다. 에드는 자신
만의 파이를 굽고 있는 건지 'sure하지 못하고' 있어요.

But I have responsibilities.   A→B

I have to win.   A→B

But was that really true?   A=B

Or was it just an excuse?   A=B

Your pies are the best.   A=B

George had said.   A↺

And Ed had been ashamed.   A=B

Because the pies he baked were really not his pies at all.   A=B

이후에도 몇 번 나오는 his pie(에드의 파이)는 아직 에드가 구워보지 못한 '자신만의 파
이'를 가리킵니다. Willy가 Bake a pie라고 말하지 않고 Bake your pie라고 말한 참된
의미를 에드는 비로소 깨달아요.

He knew his pie was not as sour or sweet as a blueberry pie.   A→B

It was different.   A=B

이 문장의 It도 아직 구워보지 못한 '에드 자신만의 파이'를 일컫습니다.

**It was different from anything else, and that was what frightened him — had
frightened him, perhaps, for his entire life.**   A=B, and A=B

그 that은 문장 첫머리에서 쉼표까지를 가리키는 대역입니다.

But he had found out that he was not the only one different.　　A→B

p.25

found out(발견하다)한 것은 무엇일까요? 답은 that 이하입니다.

Willy was different.　　A=B

Frank was different.　　A=B

Everyone who lived on Ghost Avenue was different.　　A=B

Ed closed his eyes.　　A→B

He thought about Jeremy and what he had said.　　A→B

He thought about George.　　A→B

And mostly, he thought about Willy .　　A→B

Go, son.　　(A)↻

Bake your pie.　　(A)→B

When he opened his eyes again, Ed was still looking up at the balloon in the sky .　　A=B

It was now high up in the clouds.　　A=B

The Ferris wheel continued its silent, slow movement.　　A→B

You're going to be late again.　　A=B

You're going to fail.　　A=B

The voice inside of him spoke again, but for the first time in his life, Ed ignored it.　　A↻, but A→B

it은 에드의 내면에서 들려오는 소리를 가리키는 대역입니다.

The balloon had disappeared far off in the clouds.　　A↻

It was time to bake his pie.　　A=B

George was really getting worried when the clock read 2:55 and Ed still hadn't returned to the booth.　　A=B and A↻

p.26

All the contestants were already in place, ready to begin.   A=B

George was about to go look for Ed when Ed burst through the back door and
    came running up to him.   A=B

"Sorry. I lost track of time.   불완전한 문장   A→B
    track이란 '정해진 궤도'를 말합니다. '시간의 궤도를 잃어버렸다'란 말은 '시간 가는 줄
    몰랐다'란 의미예요. 생각에 잠겨 있다가 문득 정신을 차려보니 시간이 한참 지나버린 경
    우에 쓰이는 표현입니다.

How's the oven?"   A=B

"Red-hot and ready to go," George said with a smile.   A→B
    ready to go는 'go할 준비가 되어 있다'입니다. 경쾌한 여운을 남기는 표현으로 의욕을
    불어넣어주지요.

"Okay. Get everything out of that shopping bag," Ed said, pointing to a bag on
    the floor.   A→B

"I'll get myself ready."   A→B=B'
    조금 변형된 표현입니다. 일반적으로는 I'll get the oven ready처럼 사물에 대해 쓰이지
    만 대신 '자신'을 넣어서 에드의 결연한 의지를 보여줍니다.

While Ed grabbed an apron and wrapped a bandanna around his head,
    George dug into the shopping bag.   A↺

He stopped when he took out a yellow bottle.   A↺

"Uh... Ed!" George yelled in astonishment.   A→B

"This isn't blueberry."   A=B

George showed Ed the bottle of mustard he held in his hand.   A→B/B'

"I know," Ed replied in a confident voice.   A→B

p.27

"Oh..." George mumbled in a dumbfounded way and started placing the
    bottle on the table.   A→B and (A)→B

But he turned around a second time.   A↺

124

turn around에는 갑자기 휙 뒤를 돌아보는 이미지가 있습니다. 천천히 뒤를 바라볼 때
는 look behind를 써요.

"No! Ed!   불완전한 문장   불완전한 문장

You don't understand, man!   A↩

There's a bottle of *mustard* in here!"   A=B

"George," Ed looked George straight in the eye and smiled.   A→B and (A)↩

"I know."   A↩

George took a step back, fumbled with the bottle, and opened his mouth
    halfway.   A→B, (A)→B and (A)→B

"Uh-oh. You're not going to..."   불완전한 문장   A=B
    조지의 대화문은 도중에 끝나고 말았지만 아마도 going to make that mustard pie라
    고 말하고 싶었던 게 아닐까요.

Ed finished tying the bandanna on his head, rolled up his sleeves, and
    grabbed a cutting knife.   A→B, (A)→B and (A)→B

It was one minute to three o'clock.   A=B

"I promised Willy I would go back and bake my pie. That's what I'm going to
    do," Ed said to George.   A→B

"I'm going to bake *my* pie."   A=B

George saw a genuine smile come over Ed's face as he spoke.   A→B=B'

Ed seemed relaxed for the first time today.   A=B

George still thought mustard pie wasn't a good idea, but he was happy that
    Ed was smiling again, and that was enough for George.
    A→B, but A=B, and A=B   두 번째 that은 Ed was smiling again을 가리키는 대역
    입니다.

He just nodded and put the mustard on the table.   A↩ and (A)→B

And that was when the bell rang, and the battle of the pies began for the
    second and final time.   A=B, and A↩
    이 that은 '벨이 울린 때'를 가리키는 시간의 대역입니다. 벨이 울린 때는 조지가 머스

터드를 탁자에 올려놓은 바로 그 순간이에요. 이해하기 어려우면 at that moment, the bell rang으로 읽어보세요.

p.28

"Father! Just this once!" Jeremy shouted into the cell phone.   A→B

"All I ask is... Father? Father!"   A=(B)   불완전한 문장   불완전한 문장

His father had hung up.   A⤴

Jeremy threw the cell phone at the wall of the trailer.   A→B

"Damn it!"   (A)→B

He stood up, grabbed the counter, and shoved it over.   A⤴, (A)→B, and (A)→B

All the supplies on the table crashed to the floor.   A⤴

A few people in the audience noticed this and jumped in alarm.
A→B and (A)⤴   알람이라면 보통 자명종 시계를 가장 먼저 떠올리지만 본래 alarm 이란 '위험경보'를 말합니다. 자명종 시계는 '늦잠'이란 위험을 미리 알려주는 alarm이 라고 볼 수 있어요.

"Boss? What happened? Boss!?" Jeremy's assistant cried out in surprise.   A→B

Jeremy ignored him and jumped down from the trailer.   A→B and (A)⤴

He meant to just walk straight out of the main tent.   A→B
meant는 mean의 변형입니다. '의미하다'란 뉘앙스가 있는 단어지만 바뀔 가능성이 없는 생각을 나타낼 때도 쓰여요. 이 문장에서 제레미는 텐트에서 틀림없이 나올 예정입니다.

He was sick and tired of being himself, Jeremy Lightfoot Jr., son of the millionaire.   A=B
sick and tired가 두 번째로 나왔네요. being himself는 '자신의 처지가 지겨워졌다'는 제레미의 기분을 잘 드러낸 표현이지만, 이해하기 어려우면 being을 건너뛰고 읽으세요. 일반적으로 being은 직업 등에 쓰여요(예: being a doctor). 제레미로서는 '대부호의 아 들, 제레미 Jr.'라는 꼬리표가 뗄래야 뗄 수 없는 숙명이군요. 그만둘래야 그만둘 수 없는 직업과 마찬가지인 셈입니다.

He was just one step away from the back door when a voice called out to him.
　　A=B

"Jeremy!"　　불완전한 문장

Jeremy stopped with his hands on the door.　　A↺

The voice came from the stands above him.　　A↺

"Jeremy! Don't go! Jeremy!"　　불완전한 문장　　(A)↺　　불완전한 문장

The voice cried out again.　　A↺

A very young voice.　　불완전한 문장

Voices, actually — because now his name was shouted from all over the
　　stands above.　　A=B

Jeremy quietly looked up.　　A↺

p.29

"Jeremy! You're the greatest!"　　불완전한 문장　　A=B

"Jeremy! Are you okay? Jeremy!"　　불완전한 문장　　A=B　　불완전한 문장

Twenty or thirty children were crammed overhead in the stands, cheering
　　and shouting.　　A=B

They had realized something was wrong, and had gathered above the Zombie
　　Pies trailer.　　A→B, and (A)↺

One of them started singing the Zombie Pies song and they all joined in.
　　A→B and A↺

" ♪*In the middle of the night, it's a heck of a fright*!　　A=B
　　강조를 나타내는 hell과 비슷한 의미의 heck입니다. 하지만 hell보다는 강도가 약해요.

'Cause the Zombie's in the kitchen and your stomach is all itchin'.
　　A=B and A=B　　itchin'은 본래 itching입니다. 노래의 리듬감을 살리기 위해 원래 거
　　의 발음되지 않는 g를 생략한 거예요.

So get out of that door, make your life a roar...　　(A)↺, (A)→B=B'

Go to Zombie Pies! Go to Zombie Pies! ♪"   (A)↺   (A)↺

Jeremy lowered his eyes, but the singing continued.   A→B but A↺

He stayed that way, waiting for them to stop, but they kept on singing and singing.   A↺, but A→B

"Ahhh, you meddling brats!" Jeremy still had his head down, but he spoke in a low, fiendish voice.   불완전한 문장   A→B=B', but A↺
제레미의 대화문은 but 뒤에 나오는 문장의 B 상자로도 생각할 수 있습니다.

When he raised his head, he had a pair of fake Dracula teeth in his mouth.
A→B

p.30

"You dare speak that way to the Zombie Lord!?   A↺

The Zombie Lord is always triumphant!"   A=B

The kids cheered in delight.   A↺

Jeremy gave a monster-like laugh and walked back up the stairs into the trailer.   A→B and (A)↺

Once he was safely inside, he threw away the fake teeth and grabbed an apron.   A→B and (A)→B

He shouted to his assistant.   A↺

"Forget everything.   (A)→B

We're going to Plan B.   A=B

I'm doing *Inferno*."   A=B

"Sir!?" Now the assistant was really upset.   불완전한 문장   A=B

"But that pie is dangerous!   A=B

You nearly burned yourself to death when you tried it in the lab!"   A→B
nearly는 '가까이'란 의미로 '어떻게'에 해당하는 부록입니다. death(죽음)에 가까이 다가갈 만큼 화상을 입었다고 말하며 과장하고 있어요. nearly to death는 일종의 관용구로 우리말의 '~해서 죽을 뻔하다'와 비슷한 표현이에요.

"I don't care. Get the marshmallows ready," Jeremy shouted as he spread flour on the surface of his counter.　A→B

"I'll get the blowtorch from the truck."　A→B

But before he got started, Jeremy took a glance towards Ed, and then over at Billy Bob, who stood behind the trailer.　A→B

Maybe he couldn't win at his father's game, but he still had his own way of playing.　A↺, but A→B

게임 하나에도 다양한 전술이 있습니다. 비록 아버지가 설정한 게임일지라도 play 방법은 스스로 결정하겠다고 제레미는 결심합니다.

And the game wasn't over yet.　A=B

"Okay, pie-lovers! I'm Robert R. Silverman!　불완전한 문장　A=B p.31

We're back again for the relaunch of the PIEGAMES!"　A=B

The television broadcast has already ended, so you folks here will be the only witnesses to the outcome today.　A↺, so A=B

"It's five minutes past three and we're back on track with the rematch of the PIEGAMES!"　A=B and A=B

back on track은 '궤도로 돌아오다'입니다. 이 문장에서는 '콘테스트가 정상적으로 진행되고 있다', 즉 정상궤도로 돌아왔다는 의미로 쓰였어요.

Two crowd favorites, Zombie Pies and Brown Butters are off to a quick start.

A=B　favorite은 '인기 있는 대상'을 가리켜요. 많은 참가자 중에서도 Zombie Pies와 Brown Butters가 특히 인기가 많은 모양입니다. off는 '이탈'이란 뉘앙스를 지닌 단어로 지금처럼 우위를 선점하면서 기세 좋게 출발점을 떠나가는 참가자들의 모습을 표현했어요. 이미지를 형상화하기 위해 쓰였으므로 이해하기 어려우면 건너뛰고 읽어도 상관없습니다.

Zombie Pies looks especially busy.　A=B

They're using a giant mixer to beat something up.   A=B

"Meanwhile, across the stadium from Zombie Pies you'll find Ed Wishbone
and his faithful partner 'the Tux'!   A→B

Too bad they weren't able to complete their pies this morning."   A=B
Too bad 앞에 It is를 붙이면 완전한 문장이 돼요. 무엇이 too bad한지는 they 이하를 보
면 알 수 있습니다.

"Well, what's this?   A=B

Mr. Wishbone seems to have changed his recipe this time... and... oh my
God, Ed!   A=B

What the hell are you doing!?"   A=B

Ed poured a bottle of mustard into a hot saucepan right in front of the host.
A→B

The mustard instantly bubbled and a sharp smell rose into the air.
A↺ and A↺

"I'm sorry to tell you this, Ed, but I think you've made a terrible mistake."
A=B, but A→B

The host spoke to Ed with a sour face.   A↺

"Oh man, *that* is not blueberry.   A=B

It isn't even blue!"   A=B

Half of the audience laughed.   A↺

The other half frowned as they smelled the burning odor of mustard.   A↺

Ed ignored the banter and stayed focused on his saucepan.   A→B and (A)↺
focused 이하는 '어떻게' stayed했는지 나타내는 부록입니다.

He grabbed a bottle of lemon juice and mixed in several spoonfuls of the
liquid.   A→B and (A)→B

spoonful은 '한 스푼 가득'이에요. several이 붙었으므로, '몇 스푼'을 섞었다는 의미입니다.

The host seemed a bit irritated that **Ed was not listening to him.**
    A=B that A=B

"Oh man, Ed! A *mustard* pie?   불완전한 문장   불완전한 문장

  I feel sorry for the judges."   A⤸

Ed kept working.   A→B   p.33

With quick movements, **he added half a cup of honey, a few spices, and a bag of cottage cheese** to the pan.   A→B

Then **he tossed** in a big bowl of graham crackers that George had crushed, and **stirred the entire mixture** with a large wooden spoon.
    A→B, and (A)→B   that에서 쉼표까지는 graham crackers를 꾸며주는 화장문입니다.

"Uhhm... **that looks** almost like food if you..."   A=B
    에드의 파이가 '거의 food처럼 보인다'며 사회자가 놀리고 있어요.

That was the moment a rich spicy aroma rose up out of the saucepan and reached the host's nose.   A=B
    여기서의 That은 '사회자의 말이 끊긴 순간'을 가리키는 대역입니다. a rich spicy aroma 이하는 moment를 꾸며주는 화장문이에요.

The host's high-speed patter slowed down for the first time today as he inhaled the sweet and sour smell of Ed's recipe.   A⤸

Some of the laughter from the audience also **died** down.   A⤸

They finally **noticed the serious, determined look** on Ed's face.   A→B

Ed threw a splash of red wine into the pan.   A→B

The wine caught fire and burned high for a moment.   A→B and (A)⤸

The mouth-watering smell grew even richer in the air.   A⤸

mouth-watering은 '입에 물을 주다' 다시 말해 '침을 흘리다'란 의미입니다. 우리말에도 '군침이 돌다'란 표현이 있지요.

Suddenly, the barrel oven, the mustard, and the tuxedo weren't as funny as before.   A=B

처음에는 드럼통 오븐과 머스터드와 턱시도가 우스꽝스럽게 보였지만, 에드와 조지가 정성껏 파이를 만들고 먹음직스런 파이 향까지 풍기자 관객들 눈에도 전처럼 우습게 보이지 않은 모양이에요.

p.34

"George! The crust!" Ed shouted to George as the audience watched.   A→B

George dashed to the oven.   A↺

He took out a beautiful golden-brown crust from inside.   A→B

It too gave off a slight smell of mustard.   A→B

또다시 '이탈'을 뜻하는 off가 나왔어요. 건너뛰고 읽어도 되지만 머스터드 향이 널리 퍼져나가는 장면을 그려보세요.

Spicy, but sweet.   불완전한 문장

The host cleared his throat and spoke in a somewhat lowered tone.

A→B and (A)↺   cleared his throat은 '침이나 가래 등을 뱉어 목구멍을 깨끗이 하다'란 뉘앙스를 지녀요. 우리말의 '헛기침'에 해당합니다. somewhat은 '다소'라는 뜻인데 파악하기 애매한 단어로 건너뛰고 읽어도 큰 영향은 없어요.

"Well, okay.   불완전한 문장

Let's see how the other contestants are doing.   (A)→B

Here in the next booth, we have the famous Buffi Brothers..."   A→B

The host started walking away to the next booth, but **couldn't help glancing back at Ed.**   A→B, but (A)→B

다음 부스로 가려던 사회자가 에드 쪽이 신경 쓰여 glance(흘긋 보다)하지 않을 수 없었습니다. couldn't help는 glancing을 '피하는 것이 불가능했다'란 뉘앙스로 쓰였어요.

The smell was growing richer and richer, filling the whole stadium now.
A=B

p.36

"George! How are the pies?" 불완전한 문장 A=B

"Looking good! 불완전한 문장

Give them another five minutes." (A)→B/B'
them은 파이를 가리키는 대역입니다.

"Gotcha," Ed said, and George smiled. A→B, and A↻

"Anything else?" George asked. A→B

"Nope. Now we wait." 불완전한 문장 A↻

It had been a fast, yet incredibly long, hour and a half. A=B

Ed was finally able to relax and take a deep breath. A=B

That was when he saw something walk past the back door. A=B
이번에 세 번째로 나온 '(그) 순간'을 나타내는 That입니다. 지금까지와 마찬가지로 바로 앞 문장의 상황이 일어난 순간을 가리켜요. 여기서는 에드가 deep breath를 한 순간입니다.

It made him freeze. A→B=B'
it은 앞 문장에 나온 something의 대역이에요.

"Cat?" Ed rubbed his eyes. 불완전한 문장 A→B

"No. Can't be..." 불완전한 문장 불완전한 문장

Ed walked slowly to the back door and peered down the alley. A↻ and (A)↻

There was no sign of anything. A=B

He was half convinced it had just been his imagination. A=B (that) A=B
it은 something(=the cat)을 가리키는 대역입니다.

But a number of boxes and crates were lined up along the wall, and there were plenty of hiding spaces for a cat. A=B, and A=B

a number of는 수량이 많은 상태를 나타내는 표현이지만, a lot of보다는 적은 이미지입니다. 언뜻 봐서는 얼마나 있는지 알기 힘든 수량을 표현할 때 쓰여요.

"Ed, where you goin'?" George asked with a worried look as Ed took a step out the back door. A→B

이 문장의 look은 '보다'란 화살표가 아니라 '표정'이란 의미로 쓰였어요.

"Nowhere... Just getting some fresh air," he answered. A→B

p.37

"Come back soon, man! (A)↺

The pie's almost finished." A=B

"Sure," Ed replied, but he was focused on movement in the back alley. A→B, but A=B

"Cat... You're not there, are you? Cat?" 불완전한 문장 A=B 불완전한 문장

Ed whispered as he walked past a pile of boxes. A↺

Nothing was there but some trash. A=B

He reached the end of the alley and opened the emergency exit to look outside. A→B and (A)→B

There was only an empty field beyond it. A=B

He sighed with relief. A↺

At that exact moment, Billy Bob stepped out from behind Ed and grabbed him by the neck. A↺ and (A)→B

by the neck은 앞에서도 나왔던 by the arm과 같은 형태입니다.

In a moment of panic, Ed tried to loosen Billy Bob's grip, but Billy Bob was much, much stronger. A→B, but A=B

"Give up. Quit the game. *Now*," Billy Bob whispered. A→B

Ed kept clawing at Billy Bob's hands. A→B

But it was no use. A=B

no use는 '쓸 수 없었다' 다시 말해 '소용없었다'란 뜻입니다.

He choked and gasped as Billy Bob tightened his grip further.   A↺ and (A)↺

Ed's face was starting to turn blue.   A=B

마치 휙 회전이라도 하듯이 순식간에 변하는 것을 종종 turn을 써서 표현합니다. 에드의 안색도 순식간에 파랗게 변했어요.

p.38

"**Stop! Goddammit! Stop!**   (A)↺   불완전한 문장   (A)↺

You're going to kill him!"   A=B

Someone hit Billy Bob in the back with a gasoline can.   A→B

Billy Bob grabbed the intruder and slammed him against the boxes near Ed.
A→B and (A)→B

There was a mild expression of surprise on his face when he saw that it was
his boss's son.   A=B

감정이 좀처럼 얼굴에 드러나지 않는 빌리 밥. 여기서도 다소 놀라긴 했지만 표정에는 mild한 변화만 나타났습니다.

Jeremy scrambled to his knees and shouted at Billy Bob.   A↺ and (A)↺

"**You stop this right now or I'll call the police.**"   A→B or A→B

Billy Bob ignored Jeremy and turned to Ed again.   A→B and (A)↺

"**I'm not going to quit,**" Ed said abruptly.   A→B

**His legs were shaking badly with fear, and he he was almost in tears, but he
went on anyway.**   A=B, and A=B, but A↺

went on(go on)은 활용도가 높은 표현입니다. continue와 같은 의미로, 무언가를 계속하는 상황을 가리켜요. 이 문장에서는 에드가 '말하기'를 계속했습니다.

"**They're waiting for me back on Ghost Avenue.**   A=B

I can't quit."   A↺

**Ed was trying really hard to stand up straight, but his thin, weak legs refused
to hold him up.**   A=B, but A→B

일어서려고 아무리 애써도 에드의 연약한 다리로는 체중을 up한 상태로 hold하기가 무리인 듯하네요.

Billy Bob didn't hesitate.   A↻

He moved towards Ed.   A↻

Only moments before Billy Bob's hands reached Ed, a low purr came from **the ground below.**   A↻

p.39

All three looked down.   A↻

Mr. Jones had finally found its way back and was brushing its side against Jeremy's leg.   A→B and (A)=B
way back은 '돌아갈 길'이란 뜻입니다. found는 find(발견하다)의 변형으로 '돌아갈 길을 find했다'란 말은 무사히 돌아왔다는 뜻이에요.

It went over to Billy Bob and started rolling around on his shoes, purring all the while.   A↻ and (A)→B
all the while은 '그동안'입니다. while은 언제부터 언제까지냐 하면 미스터 존스가 일련의 행동을 취한 시간을 말해요.

Billy Bob watched this through his dark sunglasses.   A→B

The two pie bakers continued to huddle on the ground while the cat went on rolling.   A→B

A long, awkward moment passed.   A↻

Billy Bob shook his head.   A→B

"You," he said to Ed.   A→B

"You need more spice."   A→B

Ed kept quiet, not knowing what to say.   A→B
쉼표 뒷부분은 원래 Ed didn't know what to say입니다. what to say는 '해야만 했던 어떤 말'이에요.

He was still recovering his breath.   A=B

He didn't know whether Billy Bob was referring to him or his pie.   A→B

refer(ring)는 우리말에는 없는 단어입니다. 굳이 번역하면 '언급하다'예요. 빌리 밥이 '톡 쏘는 맛이 더 필요해'라고 한 말이, '에드 자신'과 '에드의 파이' 중 어느 쪽에 관한 refer인지 에드는 알 수 없었어요.

Billy Bob turned to Jeremy.   A↩

"And you. It's Ms.! Not Mr.!   불완전한 문장   A=B   불완전한 문장

Mr.나 Ms.가 이름에 붙는 등장인물이라면······?

Next time, *check*, you stupid brat!"   (A)↩

Having said that, Billy Bob took a long breath.   A→B

p.40

He looked at the bewildered faces of the two, shook his head again, and walked off without another word.   A→B, (A)→B, and (A)↩

Ed and Jeremy stared at each other.   A→B

"What... what was that all about?" Jeremy murmured.   A→B

that은 방금 전 빌리 밥이 말한 이해할 수 없는 대화문 전체를 가리키는 대역입니다.

"I have no..."   A→B

Ed suddenly remembered the time and grabbed Jeremy's arm.
A→B and (A)→B

He took a quick look at Jeremy's watch.   A→B

He gasped, and hurried to his feet.   A↩, and (A)↩

Still shaking, he ran back to his booth on weak legs.   A↩

Left alone with Mr. Jones, Jeremy sat there for a while, mumbling something to himself.   A↩

Left는 leave(남다)의 변형으로, '왼쪽'을 의미하는 Left가 아니에요. 멍하니 있는 중에 고양이와 함께 제레미가 남겨졌다는 의미입니다.

Then, suddenly — he understood what Billy Bob had said.   A→B

제레미가 이해한 내용은 what 이하입니다.

Jeremy grabbed Mr. Jones and raised the cat up in the air.   A→B and (A)→B

Mr. Jones relaxed and purred.   A↷ and (A)↷

A moment later, Jeremy's eyes opened wide with surprise.   A↷

p.41

Fifteen more minutes.   불완전한 문장

George had to make a choice.   A→B

> 영어에서 choice(선택)는 주어진 상황 내에서 무언가를 고르는 것이 아니라 make 즉 만들어가는 어떤 것이라고 생각합니다. 그러므로 make a choice가 '선택을 만들어가다' 즉 '선택하다'란 의미가 돼요. 운명은 스스로 개척해나가는 것이라고 믿는 사람의 진취적인 사고방식이 잘 드러나는 표현이지요.

The rims of the pie were already a bit too brown.   A=B

In a few seconds, it would be too late.   A=B

> In a few seconds는 '앞으로 몇 초만 지나면'이란 뜻이에요. it은 익숙한 시간의 대역으로, It is one o'clock은 현재 시간이 one o'clock이란 의미입니다. It is too late은 이대로 가면 too late(때늦은)한 시간이 되고 만다는 의미예요.

Ed had not come back and it was up to him to rescue the pies.

> A↷ and A=B   it은 뒷부분의 to rescue the pies를 가리키는 대역입니다. 파이를 구하는 책임이 조지에게 up to했어요.

He was scared to do anything, but he knew in his heart that if he didn't get the pies out now, they would burn.   A=B, but A→B

> 조지가 knew한 사실은 무엇일까요? if 이하가 발생하면 they(pies)가 타버리는 것을 말합니다.

So he took a deep breath, prayed that he was doing what was right, and pulled out the two pies.   A→B, (A)→B, and (A)→B

> what was right은 '올바른 일'이란 뜻이에요. 자신은 없어도 '파이를 지금 바로 오븐에서 꺼내는 일'이 맞다고 믿고 조지는 행동에 옮겼어요.

As George was laying the two pies on the table, a wheezy Ed came tumbling into the booth behind him.   A↷

"George, are the pies okay?"   A=B

"Ed! God! I was so worried, man!   불완전한 문장   불완전한 문장   A=B

I didn't know what to do!"   A→B

Ed looked at the pies on the table and sighed with relief.   A→B and (A)↺

"George. Thanks.   불완전한 문장   불완전한 문장

You were great. Now, c'mon, let's finish.   A=B (A)↺, (A)↺

We only have ten more minutes."   A→B

p.42

"Gotcha!" George replied and handed Ed the decorations they had made
from sugar and marzipan.   A→B and (A)→B/B'
they 이하의 문장은 decorations의 화장문입니다.

Ed was about to place the first one on the pie when he suddenly stopped.
A=B   one은 decoration 중의 하나를 나타내는 대역입니다.

"Something wrong?" George asked.   A→B

"No," Ed said. "It's just..."   A→B   A=(B)

The pie was beautiful the way it was.   A=B
the way it was는 '있는 그대로'라는 의미의 관용구입니다.

It had only a simple golden-yellow surface, but the color was beautiful.
A→B, but A=B

Ed hesitated.   A↺

He looked around the arena at the other booths.   A→B

Most of the pies were finished.   A=B

They were all decorated with splendid colors, looking more like works of art
than food.   A=B
works of art는 '예술작품'이에요.

The whole arena was also much like the pies.   A=B

All colorful, glamorous, and wonderful.　불완전한 문장

But as he stood there looking around, it all suddenly **seemed strange** to Ed.
　　A=B

For a few seconds, all of the sound and racket faded into the distance, and **Ed could see** for the first time — without any distraction — the whole scene of the contest before him.　　A↺, and A→B

> before는 '전에'란 의미를 나타내는 단어로 시간을 나타낼 때 자주 쓰이지만 장소를 나타낼 때도 쓰입니다. 여기서는 에드의 '눈 앞'을 가리켜요.

p.43

And **it seemed strange.**　A=B

It seemed like he was lost in a world he didn't know.　A=B

> he was 이하를 독립된 이퀄문으로 생각하면 B 상자에 lost가 들어갑니다. 없어진 것은 자신, 즉 미아가 되었다는 말이에요.

He remembered his mother's pie.　A→B

So simple, so beautiful.　불완전한 문장

He remembered the fake apple pie he had made that first morning on Ghost Avenue.　A→B

It was simple too.　A=B

Maybe not beautiful, but simple and warm.　불완전한 문장

Ed quietly **put the decorations** back down.　A→B

He said to George, "Let's leave it this way."　A→B

> 파이를 '이 방법대로 남겨두자' 다시 말해 '이대로 두자'입니다.

George gasped.　A↺

"Why?! Ed!　불완전한 문장　불완전한 문장

Are you out of your mind?　A=B

Look at all the other pies, man!"　(A)→B

Ed smiled.　A↺

"This is our pie.　A=B

It has to be simple."　A→B
It은 앞 문장에 나오는 our pie의 대역이에요.

George was dumbfounded for a moment, but he looked at the decorations, p.44
then at Ed, then at the barrel oven, and then finally, at himself.
A=B, but A→B

"I... I guess you're right," George said.　A→B

"There ain't no decorations on Ghost Avenue, you know."　A=B
조지의 대화문은 조금 문법이 변형되었습니다. 원래는 There aren't any decorations
on Ghost Avenue예요.

That made them both smile.　A→B=B'
That은 바로 앞에 나온 조지의 대화문을 가리키는 대역입니다.

Ed added a simple ring of yellow whipped cream around the rims of the pies,
then handed the two pies to George.　A→B, then (A)→B
반지를 ring이라고 하지만 '고리 모양의 원형'은 모두 ring입니다. 여기서는 파이 테두리
를 따라 원형으로 그린 노란 휘핑크림을 가리켜요.

George went running to the judges' booth.　A↺

Jeremy walked out of the Zombie Pies trailer almost at the same time.　A↺

His assistant was rolling a giant carrier.　A=B

Ed and Jeremy's eyes met across the arena.　A↺

A few minutes later, the bell rang for the second time, and the PIEGAMES
were officially over.　A↺, and A=B

p.45

"Good evening!　불완전한 문장

This is Glen Hamperton reporting for the evening news.　A=B

We're back at the state pie festival!　A=B

Hundreds have called us insisting that we follow up on the rematch of the contest...　A→B

첫머리의 Hundreds는 Hundreds of people의 줄임형으로 TV 시청자들을 가리킵니다. 그 시청자들이 insist한 것이 that 이하이고, we는 TV 방송국의 대역입니다. 느닷없이 콘테스트 중계가 중단되어서 TV 방송국에 항의전화가 빗발친 모양이에요.

Well, here we are with a special live report, just in time for the finale."
A=B　finale 시간에 in했다. 즉 '시간을 지켰다'는 의미입니다.

"The baking is all finished.　A=B

The contestants are now presenting their pies to the audience.　A=B

The local Chinese favorite, 'Sugar & Spice,' has just finished their mystic oriental dragon dance... and now Goo Goo Planet is up on stage.
A→B... and A=B

Something like a flying saucer is landing in the middle of the stage."
A=B

p.46

"Uhm... too bad.　불완전한 문장

The audience doesn't like them too much.　A→B

Frankly, I don't blame them.　A→B

Thank God... it seems to be over now."　(A)→B... A=B
여기서의 it은 Goo Goo Planet의 진부한 쇼를 가리켜요.

"Only a few contestants seem to be left, and... oh-oh, a weird drum beat has just started up in the arena...　A=B, and, A↺

Is that..."　A=(B)

"Yes! It is!　불완전한 문장　A=(B)

Ladies and gentlemen, you're all in luck, because we're just in time for the big show!   A=B, because A=B

luck(운)이 있는 상태에 in했다는 말은 '운이 좋다'는 의미입니다.

Here they come!   A↺

Get ready!"   (A)→B

"*ZOMBIE PIES!!*"   불완전한 문장

A cloud of red smoke began to fill the arena as a low beating of drums sounded inside the tent.   A→B

p.47

The smoke suddenly parted in the middle, and Jeremy appeared from within the cloud.   A↺, and A↺

The Gravedigger followed behind him, carrying a huge tray with a blue velvet cloth spread over it.   A↺

with 이하는 tray를 꾸며주는 화장문입니다.

Red spotlights from the top of the Zombie Pies trailer flew around Jeremy as the volume of the music stepped up.   A↺

"Behold!! The fiery gates of the Inferno!"   (A)↺   불완전한 문장

Behold란 단어는 현대 영어에서는 거의 사용되지 않습니다. 이처럼 연출된 쇼에서만 종종 등장하는 과장된 호칭으로, '보라!'라고 말하면서 뭔가 대단한 볼거리에 주의를 끌려고 할 때 쓰여요. 여기서는 기껏해야 제레미의 파이지만······.

Jeremy shouted and drew the velvet cloth from the tray.   A↺ and (A)→B

A huge pie that resembled a red forest in a snow-covered land appeared from under the cloth.   A↺

Jeremy raised his hand and the music suddenly stopped.   A→B and A↺

p.48

The Gravedigger placed the tray on a stand and hurried away.

A→B and (A)↺

The audience fell silent, staring at Jeremy and his pie.　　A↺

After standing absolutely still for a moment, **Jeremy waved his hand** at the
　　pie.　　A→B

A giant blaze of fire burst out from under his cape.　　A↺

It covered the surface of the pie in flames for a few seconds, then
　　disappeared as suddenly as it had appeared.　　A→B, then (A)↺
　　이 문장에 나온 두 개의 it은 모두 A giant blaze of fire의 대역입니다.

After the fire, **the soft, marshmallow-white surface of the pie had been**
　　toasted a delicious golden-brown.　　A=B
　　구운 빵을 일컬어 토스트라고 하지만, 사실은 '노르스름하게 굽다'라는 의미의 화살표
　　toast에서 파생됐어요.

The forest had melted into a spectacular mound of red toffee.　　A↺
　　파이 위에 설탕 공예로 빨간 숲을 만들었지만 고열로 인해 녹아내려 마시멜로의 표면에
　　흘러버렸습니다. 그래서 토피(설탕, 버터, 땅콩 등을 섞어 만든 캔디)라 불리는 쫀득쫀득
　　한 캐러멜처럼 되었어요. 참고로 토피는 미국에서 캔디와 캐러멜에 버금가는 대중적인
　　과자입니다. 색깔은 대개 갈색이에요.

The crowd applauded intensely as Jeremy took a bow.　　A↺

p.49

Meanwhile, behind the stage.　　불완전한 문장

"Ed. You all right, man!"　　불완전한 문장　　불완전한 문장

"I don't know."　　A↺

"You're up next."　　A=B
　　이해하기 어려우면 You're up on stage next로 생각해보세요. 차례가 돌아오는 것을 종
　　종 You're up이라고 표현합니다. 줄지어 앉아 있는 사람들 중에서 차례가 돌아온 사람만
　　일어서는 상황을 상상해보면 이해하기 쉬울 거예요.

Ed nodded.　　A↺

George looked around the stands surrounding them, and said in a weak
 voice.　A⤴, and (A)⤴

"Man, I'd be scared if I was you."　A=B
　만약 내가 에드와 같은 상황에 처했다면…… 하고 조지가 걱정하고 있습니다.

"George, I *am* scared," Ed assured him.　A→B

"Ed Wishbone, will you please come to the stage!"　A⤴

The voice from the speakers called his name.　A→B

"That's you," George said.　A→B

Ed just nodded again and started walking towards the stage.　A⤴ and (A)→B

His legs were stiff as sticks.　A=B
　에드의 다리는 긴장해서 마치 stick처럼 되어버렸습니다.

On the last moment, George remembered to hand Ed something.　A→B
　뒷부분의 to hand Ed something을 이해하기 어려우면 handed something to Ed로
　바꿔서 읽어보세요.

Ed took it and opened his hand.　A→B and (A)→B

Willy's fortune cookie lay in his palm.　A⤴

Ed took a deep breath, and managed a smile.　A→B, and (A)→B

"Thanks, George. I'll try my best."　불완전한 문장　A→B

Jeremy was just coming down from the stage.　A=B

p.50

Ed and Jeremy's eyes met as they passed each other.　A⤴

"Your turn," Jeremy said.　A→B

It was only a whisper.　A=B

He was holding his right hand inside his cape.　A=B

Ed noticed it was burned pretty badly.　A→B

it은 제레미의 right hand를 가리키는 대역입니다. pretty에는 '예쁜, 귀여운' 이외에 '꽤'
라는 의미가 있으므로 제레미의 화상이 꽤 심한 상태라는 것을 알 수 있어요.

Jeremy's assistant came rushing up to him with a bucket of ice water as soon
as Jeremy sat down.　A⤵

Jeremy dipped his hand in the bucket and **grunted** with pain.　A→B and (A)⤵

"Ed Wishbone? **Are you there?**"　불완전한 문장　A=B

The announcer called out again.　A⤵

Ed walked out onto the stage.　A⤵

A spotlight came searching for him.　A⤵

As the spotlight guided him to the center of the stage, **Ed was surprised to**
hear a lot of clapping coming from the audience.　A=B

He saw a microphone waiting for him.　A→B

His pies were there too, displayed on a table.　A=B
쉼표 이하는 '어떻게'에 해당하는 부록으로, 파이가 어떻게 됐는지 상세히 설명하고 있
어요.

He walked forward, but very stiffly.　A⤵

When he reached the microphone, **Ed took a breath** and **looked** around the
arena.　A→B and (A)⤵

Hundreds, maybe thousands of eyes fell on him.　A⤵

He swallowed.　A⤵

p.51

He tried to say something, but **his mind was** completely **blank.**
A→B, but A=B

He tried to think of something to say, anything, but **his brain** simply **refused
to work.**　A→B, but A→B
work는 폭넓게 쓸 수 있는 화살표입니다. 가장 기본적인 의미는 '정상적으로 작동하다'
인데 이 문장에서는 에드의 머리가 긴장해서 제대로 작동하지 못하고 있네요.

"Hello."　불완전한 문장

He said finally, his voice trembling a little.　A↺

A few people in the audience laughed.　A↺

"I'm Ed Wishbone.　A=B

　I used to own a pie shop.　A→B
　used to를 화살표 바로 앞에 쓰면 과거를 그리워하는 문장이 돼요. 이런 형태의 문장을
　보면 문장 전체가 세피아 톤으로 빛바랜 듯한 느낌을 상상해보세요.

　But now, I live down on Ghost Avenue."　A↺

A stir went through the crowd.　A↺

"A lot of people live there — and they're all kind to me.　A↺ and A=B

　They... they are poor. Really poor.　A=B　불완전한 문장

　It's certainly not the best place to live, but It's... It's still my home.
　A=B, but A=B

　It's the only home I have."　A=B

As he spoke, Ed felt the warmth of the campfire in the cinema.　A→B

The peaceful night sky above Ghost Avenue spread through him.　A↺
에드의 마음속에 spread한 것은 고스트 애비뉴의 평화로운 밤하늘입니다.

He opened his hands and was surprised that the sweat on his palms had
　dried.　A→B and (A)=B

He felt a little calmer than before.　A↺

"These past weeks have been a very hard time for me...　A=B　p.52
　These past weeks란 파이 혜본을 잃고 난 후 에드가 보낸 몇 주간을 가리켜요.

　But somehow, it all seems a lot more precious than the rest of my
　life.　A=B
　it은 앞 문장의 These past weeks의 대역입니다.

Weeks that I'll never forget."   불완전한 문장
that 이하는 Weeks의 화장문입니다.

A quiet rush of memories flew through Ed's mind as he said these words.
A↩

Losing his shop, running to the bank, waking up in a ghost town... everything
seemed like such a long time ago.   A=B

Ed took a long, deep breath, and continued.   A→B, and (A)↩

"Sometimes... I think the best pie isn't always sweet.   A→B

Sometimes it's not sour or bitter either.   A=B
여기서의 it은 앞 문장의 best pie를 가리키는 대역이지만 마음속 대화에 몰두하고 있는
에드는 점차 it을 '인생'을 가리키는 대역으로 썼어요. 이 문장 이후에 나오는 에드의 대
화문에서는 it이 어떤 경우에도 대역으로 쓰일 수 있다는 특징을 최대한 활용했습니다.

Sometimes... I think... I think that it can even be a mustard pie."   A→B
이해하기 어려우면 even을 건너뛰고 읽으세요.

Ed lowered his eyes to his pie.   A→B

And for a second, the words Billy Bob had said to him came back as an echo.
A↩
echo는 '메아리'지만 이 문장에서는 빌리 밥의 말이 마음속에서 '메아리처럼 반복해서
울렸다'고 비유를 들어 말하고 있습니다.

Spice. You need more spice.   불완전한 문장   A→B

"It's a little spicy at first, but we all need some spice to recognize the
sweetness hidden underneath.   A=B, but A→B

I've learned in these past few weeks that a good pie is a lot like real
life.   A→B   에드가 최근 몇 주간 learned한 것은 that 이하입니다.

Everyone's life.   불완전한 문장

p.53

I used to spend a lot of time leaning on the counter of my old pie shop, wondering why no one came to buy my pies.　　A→B

But I think I know now."　　A→B

앞 문장에 나온 '왜 아무도 내 파이를 사러 오지 않았을까'라는 의문의 reason에 대해 I know now라고 대답하고 있습니다.

The audience had become almost completely silent.　　A=B

Ed was so absorbed in his thoughts that **he didn't notice.**　　A=B that A⟳

"**I tried so hard to make good pies... great pies, but being a baker, a pie baker, isn't really about making pies...**"　　A→B, but A=B

이 문장과 다음 문장의 make를 비교해보세요. make란 단어는 물리적으로 무언가를 '만들다'뿐만 아니라 '(인간의) 행복을 만들다'와 같이 추상적인 표현에도 쓸 수 있다는 것을 알 수 있어요.

Ed took another deep breath, and said in a firm voice, "**it's about making people happy."**　　A→B, and (A)→B

it's의 it은 형태상으로는 앞 문장의 being a pie baker를 가리키는 대역이지만 동시에 파이를 만드는 것, 인생을 살아가는 것, 행복해지는 것, 사람을 행복하게 해주는 것 등······ 최근 몇 주간의 인생을 통틀어 에드의 생각까지도 포함한 it입니다. it은 여러 상황에서 대역으로 쓰이는 편리한 단어지만, 동시에 말로 표현하기 힘든 느낌을 말하려고 할 때 그 느낌을 더해 표현할 수 있는 유일한 단어이기도 해요.

The audience remained silent.　　A⟳

Ed had expected laughter, so **he felt** relieved as he whispered into the microphone.　　A→B, so A⟳

"Uh... **That's all.**　　A=B

Thank you for listening. **Thank you."**　　(A)→B　　(A)→B

The applause that came a moment later was big.　　A=B

Really big.　　불완전한 문장

And the applause continued — for a long, long time.　　A⟳

p.54

The cat walked down the center of the fairgrounds gracefully, almost dragging its full tummy on the ground.　A↻

It suddenly came to a stop when Ed stepped out of the main tent, his bandanna in one hand and an exhausted look on his face.　A↻

Ed spotted the cat immediately, but didn't seem surprised.　A→B, but (A)=B

"I thought I saw you," Ed said to the cat.　A→B

The cat cautiously retreated a few steps.　A↻

"Don't worry, the contest's almost over.　(A)↻, A=B

I'm not going to try and catch you and get my only good shirt ripped."
A=B and (A)→B=B'　한 장밖에 없는 좋은 셔츠가 고양이한테 찢김을 당하게 (ripped) 될까 봐(get) 고양이를 붙잡지 않기로 했다는 말입니다. 이해하기 어려우면 I'm not going to try, I'm not going to catch you, I'm not going to get my only good shirt ripped란 세 문장이 이어져 있다고 생각해보세요.

Ed sat down on a bench near the cat.　A↻

The cat frowned, but decided Ed was not a concern.　A↻, but (A)→B

Ed watched the glimmering lights of the carnival in silence, with the cat at his feet.　A→B
in silence(고요히)는 '어떻게' watched했는지를 나타낸 부록입니다.

The applause was still echoing back inside the arena, but it all seemed far away.　A=B, but A=B

The glamour, the importance, and the meaning of the contest felt vague to Ed as he sat there.　A↻

Ed looked at the cat.　A→B

Their eyes met for a moment.　A↻

p.55

"I used to have a fairly peaceful life, you know," Ed said softly.　A→B

"Until that day you came into my shop.　불완전한 문장

문장의 중간에 Ed said softly가 삽입되었지만 사실은 다음 문장과 이어진 하나의 대화 문장입니다. Until로 시작하는 부분은 앞 문장의 '시간'을 나타내는 부록으로 생각해주세요.

Since then, my life has been one big roller-coaster ride.   A=B

No thanks to you."   불완전한 문장

일반적으로 Thanks to you라는 감사의 인사를 하지만 여기서는 No를 붙여 비꼬는 인사를 했네요. 우리말로 하면 '겉치레 인사는 하지 않겠어'쯤이 되지 않을까요.

The cat seemed not to care.   A=B

It just yawned and continued licking its paws.   A↺ and (A)→B

"But you know what, cat?" Ed said.   A→B

"I think I'm starting to like roller coasters."   A→B

A low purr echoed a few feet away.   A↺

Ed looked up.   A↺

He saw Jeremy sneaking out of the tent with a cat cage in one hand.
   A→B=B'

Jeremy had his heavy coat on, and seemed to be leaving.   A→B, and (A)=B

on은 '접촉'을 의미하는 단어입니다. '코트에 on(접촉)하다', 다시 말해 '코트를 입다'란 의미입니다.

"Damn," Jeremy said.   A→B

"Why are you out here?"   A=B

Ed shrugged.   A↺

"What about you?"   불완전한 문장

에드가 두 문장 앞에 나온 제레미의 질문에 대해 '그럼, 너는 어떻게 된 거냐'고 되묻고 있어요.

Jeremy's cat purred again in its cage.   A↺

The Big Fat Cat opened one eye, took a look, and then closed it.
   A→B, (A)→B, and (A)→B

"I'm going home," Jeremy said.   A→B

"Why? What about the results?"   불완전한 문장   불완전한 문장

Jeremy sighed.   A↺

"I'm smart enough to know when I've lost.   A=B
자신의 영리함을 'lost했을 때 그 사실을 바로 알아차릴 만큼 영리하다'라고 비꼬아 표현했습니다. 제레미다운 시니컬한 문장이에요. 여기서 lost는 '잃다'가 아니라 '지다'란 의미로 쓰였습니다.

I just don't want to see the kids when they find out.   A→B
they는 kids의 대역입니다. kids가 find out하는 것은 Jeremy가 lost하는 장면이에요.

And your pie..."   불완전한 문장

Jeremy realized he was talking too much.   A→B

He coughed, and went on more slowly.   A↺, and (A)↺

"...Uh, nothing. Well, anyway, it's okay.   불완전한 문장   A=B

I really don't need the prize money, you know."   A→B

He shrugged.   A↺

"I'm rich."   A=B

p.56   "Ed!"   불완전한 문장

Just then, George flew out of the main tent, a look of awe on his face.   A↺

He was trying to say something, but the words seemed to be stuck in his
    mouth.   A=B, but A=B

"George."   불완전한 문장

Ed rose, worried that something had happened again.   A↺

"Is everything okay?   A=B

Did the judges reach a decision?"   A→B

George smiled, and with tears forming in his eyes, said in a warm voice.

A⤶, and (A)⤶

"Oh yeah. Yeah, they sure did."   불완전한 문장   A⤶

> did는 두 문장 앞에 쓰인 reach a decision의 대역입니다. 좀 더 알기 쉽게 쓰면 They sure did reach a decision이에요.

Jeremy shrugged as he watched Ed and George run back into the main tent, back into the growing applause.   A⤶

He said to The Cat Formerly Known As Mr. Jones, "Don't worry. I'm okay."

> A→B   빌리 밥의 지적으로 미스터란 호칭을 잃어버린 미스터 존스……. 새로운 이름을 지어주기 전까지 임시로 붙인 이름이 The Cat Formerly Known As Mr. Jones이므로 머리글자는 전부 대문자로 되어 있습니다.

Jeremy patted the cat's cage.   A→B

"C'mon, let's go home."   (A)⤶, (A)⤶

Jeremy slowly walked away into the night, whistling the theme music of Zombie Pies.   A⤶

p.57

"Willy! BeeJees! Frank!   불완전한 문장   불완전한 문장   불완전한 문장

We're back!   A=B

We've got the money!"   A→B

> the money는 당연히 파이 콘테스트에서 받은 상금을 말해요.

Ed called out as he entered the cinema.   A⤶

George was one step behind him.   A=B

The cinema lobby was almost completely dark.   A=B

Ed and George hurried through the piles of junk.   A⤶

"C'mon! There's a taxi waiting outside!   (A)⤶   A=B

I already called the hospital!"   A→B

Ed shouted louder as he approached the swinging doors.   A⤶

"I'm sorry I'm late!   A=B   A=B

We had an accident and..."   A→B
an accident는 콘테스트에서 재대결을 하게 된 바람에 늦게 돌아오게 된 상황을 가리킵니다.

Ed pushed the doors open and **stopped** short.   A→B and (A)↺
short는 '단거리나 단시간'을 일컫습니다. 즉 '문을 열고 들어서자마자 멈춰 섰다'란 의미예요.

The hall was silent.   A=B

His voice echoed in the empty space.   A↺

"Willy?"   불완전한 문장

p.60

The cinema was absolutely silent.   A=B

Step by step, **Ed** slowly **approached** Willy.   A→B

Willy was completely still.   A=B

Not only Willy, but the air around him also seemed still.   A=B

Time itself seemed still there.   A=B

Ed knew that Willy was dead.   A→B

"It was about an hour ago," **BeeJees** said.   A→B
이 문장의 It은 '윌리의 죽음'을 가리키는 대역입니다. 차마 die라는 단어를 입 밖에 내지 못하고 윌리의 죽음을 전하기 위해 it이라는 애매모호한 대역을 쓴 거예요. 여기서도 it이 '말로는 표현하기 어려운 느낌'이나 '차마 말로 표현할 수 없는 생각'을 나타내는 중요한 역할을 하고 있습니다.

He held his face in his hands, squatting against the ragged bed.   A→B

"**He** suddenly **opened his eyes** and **smiled.**   A→B and (A)↺
He는 윌리의 대역입니다. his eyes도 윌리의 눈을 가리켜요.

I thought maybe he was waking up and **I ran** over to him.   A→B and A↺

He was already dead."   A=B

"Wh... why..."   불완전한 문장

But Ed couldn't continue.   A↺

The words remained in his mouth.   A↺

He tried to swallow, but his mouth was dry.   A→B, but A=B

Willy wore a smile on his face.   A→B

He looked like he was proud of something.   A=B
처음 본 순간 윌리는 자랑스레 미소를 머금고 있었지만, 무엇을(something) 자랑스러워했는지는 아무도 알 수 없었습니다.

p.61

"I think he knew," BeeJees said as he laid his eyes on the trophy in Ed's hands.   A→B

Tears gleamed in his eyes.   A↺

"I think he knew."   A→B

Ed closed his eyes tight.   A→B

He was trembling slightly.   A=B

The light of the moon was a soft tender yellow against the darkness of the world.   A=B

It shined on Willy as if it were guiding him to a better world.   A↺
It은 앞 문장의 The light of the moon을 가리키는 대역입니다.

A world without hunger or pain or cold.   불완전한 문장
이 문장과 다음 문장은 둘 다 앞 문장의 a better world가 어떤 곳인지 구체적으로 설명하고 있습니다.

A world where he could finally rest.   불완전한 문장

A world that was not cruel like the one they had to live in.   불완전한 문장
조금 어려운 문장이네요. 첫머리의 A world는 '윌리가 가게 될 저 세상'으로, 그곳은

cruel하지 않다는 말입니다. 그럼 무엇에 비해 cruel하지 않을까요. 그 답은 the one they had to live in(one은 world의 대역)으로, they는 에드 일행, 즉 에드 일행이 살고 있는 이 세상에 비해서 cruel하지 않은 세상을 말합니다.

"I don't know how... But I..."　　A→B... 불완전한 문장

BeeJees broke down as he spoke.　　A⤴

"I... really think he knew... and I think... I think he was happy."　　A→B... A→B

The Golden Crust trophy glittered in the moonlight as **it fell** from Ed's hands, **rolled** on the floor, and **lay** still in the dark.　　A⤴ as A⤴, (A)⤴, and (A)⤴

---

p.62

The silence of the night slowly **eased the tension** of the long hard day.
　　A→B

The temperature was almost **below zero.**　　A=B

Ed's breath turned white as he walked down the dark street, the Golden Crust trophy in his hands.　　A⤴

He chose a place on the sidewalk, and **sat** looking up at the stars.
　　A→B, and (A)⤴

He watched them for a long time, as if he could find Willy among them — if he looked hard enough.　　A→B
이 문장에서 them은 둘 다 stars를 가리키는 대역입니다.

Behind Ed, **the cat played** around with the Golden Crust trophy.　　A⤴

The cat had realized it wasn't a real pie some time ago, but **it kept playing** anyway.　　A→B, but A→B
앞에 나온 it은 트로피를 가리키는 대역이고, 뒤에 나온 it은 the cat을 가리키는 대역입니다.

All the excitement of the day seemed like a dream far away as Ed sat there in the cold.　　A=B

He remembered the day he met Willy, right there on the street.　　A→B

He remembered his soft voice.   A→B

He remembered his careful words.   A→B

And most of all, he remembered his soothing smile.   A→B

"What am I going to do now, Willy?" Ed whispered into the empty space
    around him.   A→B

The words turned white and disappeared immediately.   A↷ and (A)↷

"What, Willy? *What*?"   불완전한 문장   불완전한 문장

After a long pause, Ed took the fortune cookie out of his pocket.   A→B

He stared at it for a moment, then cracked it open.   A→B, then (A)→B=B'

A thin piece of paper was inside.   A=B

Ed read it.   A→B

Most treasures are in the places you first find them.   A=B

Ed read it. over and over again, trying to find some meaning in the words.
    A→B

Some answer.   불완전한 문장

But only tears came and fell.   A↷ and (A)↷

He cuddled his knees and cried.   A→B and (A)↷

The cat just continued to play with the trophy.   A→B

Up above town, the first flakes of snow started to fall, announcing the arrival   p.63
    of a long, cold season.   A→B

A church bell rang far away in the mountains.   A↷

The snow quickly grew stronger, and soon, the town of Everville was covered
    with the color of winter.   A↷, and A=B

December 25th.   불완전한 문장

It was Christmas Day.   A=B

6권을 끝내며

Big Fat Cat 시리즈는 즐기기 위한 책입니다. 저희 스태프도 편집자도 Big Fat Cat 시리즈를 한 번도 교재라고 생각한 적은 없습니다. 그러니 읽는 동안 즐거우셨다면 그것으로 충분합니다.

다만 이 시리즈를 되돌아볼 때 다음 한 가지만큼은 기억해주셨으면 합니다. 바로 말을 하는 주체는 언제나 사람이라는 점입니다. 영어든 우리말이든, 에드가 말하든 제레미가 말하든 언제나 말을 하는 사람의 마음을 언어라는 그릇에 담아 표현한 것입니다. 언어는 달라도 음성에 담긴 말뜻은 크게 다르지 않습니다.

그러므로 영어가 서툴더라도 여기까지 온 분이라면 등장인물들의 말을 충분히 전달받았으리라고 생각합니다. 그 이유는 그들의 사정을 잘 알고 있고 그들의 기분을 이해하고 있기 때문입니다. 언어를 이해하기 위한 최대의 비결은 학습법이나 반복 훈련에 있지 않습니다. A→B도 A=B도 아닙니다. 최대의 비결은 말을 하고 있는 사람의 마음을 이해하려는 자세에 있습니다. Big Fat Cat 시리즈에서 언급한 모든 내용을 잊어버려도 괜찮습니다. 다만 마음을 이해하려는 자세만큼은 앞으로 영어를 계속 익혀가는 과정에서 늘 기억해주시길 바랍니다. 여기까지 함께한 독자 여러분에게 저희 스태프들이 드리는 마지막 부탁입니다.

이제는 딱 한 권이 남았습니다. 에드와 고양이의 종착역은 어디일까요? 그 결말을 맞이하기에 안성맞춤인 날이 다가오고 있습니다. 일 년에 한 번 기적이 용납되는 날. 12월 25일, 크리스마스! 올해 크리스마스, 눈이 내리기 시작할 때 이 이야기도 막을 내립니다.

Big Fat Cat 시리즈 마지막 작품 〈Big Fat Cat and the Snow of the Century〉에서 다시 만나기로 하지요!

Happy Reading!
Takahiko Mukoyama

이 시리즈는 영문법 교재가 아닙니다. 학습서도 아닙니다. '영어 읽기'를 최우선 목표로 삼고 쓴 책입니다. 몸으로 체험하고 느낄 수 있도록 기존 영문법과는 조금 다른 해석을 실은 부분도 있습니다. 어디까지나 이제 막 영어 읽기를 시작하는 학생들의 이해를 돕기 위해서 의도적으로 도입한 장치입니다.

STAFF

written and produced by Takahiko Mukoyama	기획 · 원작 · 글 · 해설 무코야마 다카히코
illustrated by Tetsuo Takashima	그림 · 캐릭터 디자인 다카시마 데츠오
translated by Eun Ha Kim	우리말 번역 김은하
art direction by Yoji Takemura	아트 디렉터 다케무라 요지
technical advice by Fumika Nagano	테크니컬 어드바이저 나가노 후미카
edited by Will Books Editorial Department	편집 윌북 편집부
English-language editing by Michael Keezing	영문 교정 마이클 키징
supportive design by Will Books Design Department	디자인 협력 윌북 디자인팀
supervised by Atsuko Mukoyama Yoshihiko Mukoyama	감수 무코야마 아츠코(梅光学院大学) 무코야마 요시히코(梅光学院大学)
a studio ET CETERA production	제작 스튜디오 엣세트러
published by Will Books Publishing Co.	발행 윌북

special thanks to:

Mac & Jessie Gorham
Baiko Gakuin University

series dedicated to "Fuwa-chan", our one and only special cat

Studio ET CETERA는 야마구치현 시모노세키시에서 중학교 시절을 함께 보낸 죽마고우들이 의기투합하여 만든 기획 집단입니다. 우리 스튜디오는 작가, 프로듀서, 디자이너, 웹마스터 등 다재다능한 멤버들로 구성되어 있으며 주로 출판 분야에서 엔터테인먼트와 감성이 결합된 작품을 만드는 것을 목표로 하고 있습니다.
ET CETERA라는 이름은 어떤 분류에도 속할 수 있으면서 동시에 어떤 분류에도 온전히 속하지 않는 '그 외'라는 뜻의 et cetera에서 따왔습니다. 우리들만이 할 수 있는 독특한 작품을 만들겠다는 의지의 표현이자 '그 외'에 속하는 많은 사람들을 위해 작품을 만들겠다는 소망이 담긴 이름입니다.

옮긴이 **김은하**

유년 시절을 일본에서 보낸 추억을 잊지 못해 한양대학교에서 일어일문학을 전공했다. 어려서부터 한일 양국의 언어를 익힌 덕분에 번역이 천직이 되었다. 번역하는 틈틈이 바른번역 글밥 아카데미에서 출판 번역 강의를 겸하고 있다. 주요 역서로 〈클래식, 나의 뇌를 깨우다〉, 〈지구 온난화 충격 리포트〉, 〈세계에서 제일 간단한 영어 책〉, 〈빅팻캣의 영어 수업: 영어는 안 외우는 것이다〉 등 다수가 있다.

Big Fat Cat and the Fortune Cookie
빅팻캣과 포춘 쿠키 빅팻캣 시리즈 6

펴낸날 개정판 1쇄 2018년 5월 20일
　　　　개정판 5쇄 2024년 5월 24일
글작가 무코야마 다카히코
그림작가 다카시마 데츠오
옮긴이 김은하

펴낸이 이주애, 홍영완
펴낸곳 (주)윌북
출판등록 제2006-000017호

주소 10881 경기도 파주시 광인사길 217
전자우편 willbooks@naver.com
전화 031-955-3777
팩스 031-955-3778
홈페이지 willbookspub.com
블로그 blog.naver.com/willbooks 포스트 post.naver.com/willbooks
트위터 @onwillbooks 인스타그램 @willbooks_pub

ISBN 979-11-5581-170-2 14740